ORLANDO'S NEMESIS

David Lynch Topitzer

ORLANDO'S NEMESIS. Copyright © 2007 by David Lynch Topitzer. All rights reserved. Printed in the United States of America. No part of this book may be used or reproduced in any manner whatsoever without written permission except in the case of brief quotations embodied in critical articles and reviews.

New Road Press
www.newroadpress.com

ISBN: 978-0-6151-5304-9

Cover design by Sarah Marie Toth
Cover photography by Florea Marius Catalin

For Kim, Oliver, Delia

Acknowledgments

This book has been a work in progress for over 12 years. It is difficult to be an effective high school history teacher, father two children and be a good husband while trying to write a book.

I would like to thank a number of people for reading the manuscript. Mary Jane Topitzer, Kate Erwin and Sarah Toth provided useful lay feedback. Kurt Simonds helped a great deal in flushing-out the story. Professor Lisa Wilson provided interesting feedback in regards to gender roles. Professor Tom Carty provided valuable historical insight and practical advice for making it more readable. Ellen Wicklum, editor at University Press of New England, provided both constructive criticism and encouragement. Christopher Collier has provided encouragement since the very start back in the spring of 1992 when I wrote a paper dealing with Theodore Dwight for his graduate seminar. Moreover, Kit Collier is the one who suggested I keep going; when I sent him the manuscript in the spring of 2003 I was surprised that he liked it so much.

In the end, I could have heeded more of the advice from the people mentioned above. Sometimes work must be abandoned so life can go on.

Preface

When I started graduate school I wanted more than anything to write history that would be engaging, that would be a story. That is what I have tried to do, tell a story. It is very difficult to balance the sometimes competing goals of wide readability and historical integrity. With that said, this story is mostly true. It emanates from my scholarly historical work.[1] The story is based on my historical interpretations of primary sources. Some characters and scenes etcetera, have been created to help the story along.

If you are offended in any way by my interpretations or insights I encourage you look at the same sources and come up with your own interpretations.

This work has been written largely in "pedestrian prose," in an effort to accommodate peripatetic readers.

Prologue

New York, New York, 1846

For Theodore Dwight the end was near. No matter, the sun cleared the morning dew. Women strolled in light colored dresses, holding parasols under the sun's warmth – their brown, blond and auburn hair glistening. Wafting voices and chirping birds competed. It was spring 1846. New York was a bustle then - prosperous people, commerce and trade. And also poverty, disease, crime, gangs and prostitution plagued New York, particularly after the recent wave of dirt-poor Irish coming to New York after the potato famine. Nevertheless, in this part of town, Manhattan, rambling roses tangled around white picket fences, laughing children chased stray hens, over-dressed merchants conversed and women strolled along the waterfront in peace. The smell of pine tar and linseed oil drifted up from the docks nearby. Theodore Dwight sat in his study on this warm June day, overlooking the harbor and this scene. For him, though, the end was near. He was very old, 82. Nevertheless, he still liked to sit at his desk every day, if only for an hour or two, so that he could scribble down some note, some random observation about what he had read in the morning paper. He could still warn of danger to his beloved

American republic. He saw the impending doom that the institution of slavery had wrought; the country was clearly divided - North and South - and in only a matter of time it would tear apart at the seams. Yet, his own family was thriving. His mind was now at rest and his soul soothed, despite his earlier transgressions.

Sometimes he wrote short poems late at night by the light of his Argand whale-oil lamp, nothing like the very long ones he had written and published as a young man.

And sometimes he found himself writing two simple words: "love endures."

It was his work ethic, more than anything else, which compelled him to sit down every morning and hold his feather quill in his hand. On more than one occasion his famous maternal grandfather, Jonathan Edwards, had reminded him of the necessity to work hard and long to serve the Lord God with his whole heart and mind.

He smiled as he recalled his book, *History of the Hartford Convention*, published in 1833. The Hartford Convention convened in the winter of 1814 as group of northern merchant Federalists. They sought to make demands on the Madison administration in an effort to stop the War of 1812. The New England states were reluctant to continue to provide militias for a war that would ruin their trading relationship with England. New England secession was in the air. It is a long, tedious book, complete with a list of documents showing the instructions each state had given to its delegates. He had written of the objectives of the convention: "to confer on the practicability of devising means of security and defense—that is, to perform the task which the national government had thrown upon them in 1812." In

Dwight's mind, the impression that the Hartford Convention had been a meeting to consider secession was a gross misrepresentation of the Federalists' objectives. As the convention's secretary, he thought it proper that he should be the one to set the record straight.

Theodore believed that he had served his state and country well. And his greatest service had been to try and save his country by exposing the many faults of Thomas Jefferson. In his mind, he wanted to believe that he had been precise and fair. Even late in his life he constantly recycled in his mind his views about Jefferson, which he had thought that he had laid to rest in his book, *The Character of Thomas Jefferson*. Then across the room was his bible. He wondered if his work was inspired by God.

He looked at his greatest accomplishment, which rested on the desk. *The Character of Thomas Jefferson* is over 440 pages of meticulous observations on Thomas Jefferson. Theodore had begun gathering material about Jefferson soon after the man's death in 1826. The book had been published in 1839. It left no doubt as to Jefferson's character.

Theodore had used Jefferson's letters, addresses, essays—any and everything that he could lay his hands on. Various statements, which the statesman had made over a lifetime, produced enough evidence to reveal the true nature of our third president.

Dwight believed that Jefferson's friendship with John Adams had been one of Jefferson's many pretenses. He needed the friendship of the second President to ensure that future generations would regard him highly. Additionally, Jefferson's support of the Constitution was hollow—a way to further his own political ambitions. Those ambitions had proved dangerous, for Jefferson was, at heart, a visionary and a theorist. His thinking was governed by abstract, impractical thinking—preposterous ideas that yoked freedom with revolution. Americans needed to know this.

Clearly, French society had corrupted Jefferson. He was a Deist, believing that God played no direct role in human affairs and that following biblical scripture was a waste of time. He lived opulently beyond his means, only to pass-on crushing debt to the next generation. His lifestyle was made possible by his dependence on hundreds of black slaves.

Jefferson had slept with slaves, slept with Sally Hemming as far back as his stay in France, had sired bastard children by his servants. That was an abomination. Slavery was a base enough institution to begin with, but for Jefferson to use slavery for his own immoral pleasures, was something that had always outraged Theodore.

In the final analysis, Jefferson had failed to see that the state existed to serve Christianity and the will of God. That was the greatest error in his thinking. In Dwight's mind Jefferson was an infidel.

Jefferson is the most well known of the revolutionary era because he wrote the Declaration of Independence, but more so, Dwight believed that Jefferson should be understood as the symbol of chaos, the same kind of chaos that ensued during the Revolutionary war.

Often when he wrote, Theodore would ponder this fifty-year resentment towards Thomas Jefferson.

And reliving this resentment toward Jefferson still made Dwight angry. This anger perhaps took root back when Theodore was just 13 years old.

Northampton, Massachusetts, 1777

Chapter One

It was late afternoon—pleasantly warm and dry—as thirteen year old Theodore Dwight walked through the woods near his family's farm in Northampton, Massachusetts. The year was 1777. The slanting sun dropped through a grove of maple trees, throwing broad yellow beams across Theodore's path as he moved through a hundred different shades of green beneath the forest's canopy. The smell of humus and green leaves filled the air. This was his favorite place to be since his father had left to claim land in West Florida. That had been last year, and his father hadn't returned—was *never* returning—to work the land just a hundred yards away.

Never.

A blue jay's raspy call spread out from a nearby hickory branch . . . and then the air was once again silent, almost holy. For Theodore, walking through the woods, touching its leaves and breathing the green, wooded air was far more preferable than sitting in the Congregational church each Sunday, with the droning of the preacher's voice, the timid hymns, and the endless prayers. He much preferred the shrill notes of a jay or the soft, clear song of a loon at dusk—even the sound of a busy squirrel as it rustled through dead leaves to find cover beneath a fallen trunk.

This is where he did his best thinking. Here, there were no arguments about patriotism, no squabbling by old men about loyalty to the mother country versus independence for the colonies. No views on what right-thinking men should hold in their brains. This was all the freedom that Theodore Dwight needed. He could pretend he was king of all the forest, lord of possums and raccoons and deer . . . or he could curl up and sleep, dreaming about his father's voice as it had once sounded after dinner near the living room hearth, his father smoking a long-stemmed pipe and talking of Northampton, the village he had helped shape with years of determination and hard work.

And here in the forest he could always be alone with his thoughts of Abigail Thorne, who was two years older than he and always sat in the second-to-last pew on the left side of church on Sunday mornings. She didn't wear lose-fitting smocks like the other girls. Her light blue Sunday dress was cinched at the waist, revealing the fact that Abigail indeed had an actual shape, though Theodore supposed it was considered sinful to think too long or too hard about the figure of a young girl. But Theodore was alone here, with no one to stop his recollections of how Abigail turned her head ever-so-slightly at certain points during the service, peering back into the vestibule where Theodore sat with his mother and brothers and sisters. He had never spoken with Abigail, but there was no doubt in his mind that her gaze was intended for him.

Most definitely.

*   *   *

Dwight crouched low to the ground between two

slender hickory trees. There were men coming up the road to his home, implements of some kind resting against their shoulders. They all wore knee breeches and looked a bit like a local militia, muskets cradled in their arms. It was hard to make out exactly what they carried as they trooped through the dust and the haze of the August afternoon.

And then slowly, Theodore saw plainly what the men were holding as they rounded the gentle curve in the dirt-packed road: axes, rifles, and torches.

Dwight blinked, his heart hammering in his chest, his breath coming fast and hard. He knew he should sprint from his hiding place at the edge of the woods and dash through the rows of corn, past the barn, past the tool shed and up to the main house, alerting his family to the coming danger.

But he was frozen.

The men were walking hurriedly now. It was too late to warn anyone of what was about to happen.

One of the men had already produced a long-handled knife, the kind used for gutting deer or hogs, and he was making his way to the pigs in the pen on the right side of the barn.

The rest happened quickly.

Two men—tall, with dark hair and ropey muscles—approached the barn itself and threw their torches into piles of hay and timber inside the entrance.

"Hello? Who's there?"

His mother's voice. She was standing in front of her home, two of her children gathered in the folds of her skirt.

Ungodly squeals pierced the air. The man with the long-handled knife was killing the pigs, slashing wildly at them, slitting their throats, thrusting his metal hard into the animals' sides.

Theodore Dwight wished to call out, wanted to cry "father!" But the single word was choked in his throat by the realization that his father had been killed a thousand miles away. Major Timothy Dwight would not be able to come to the aid of his family, nor his horrified son lying between two hickory trees.

"Leave!" his mother screamed. "You have no right to—"

Her words were lost in the growing chaos. Yellow flames seized the boards all across the front of the barn, the crackling and popping of dry pine filling the air. Heat waves shimmered and danced in the air, distorting the images Theodore was beholding. The August afternoon had become an ugly painting, its forms grotesquely melting under the cruel assault of this band of Patriots who were, once and for all, going to take advantage of the permanent absence of Major Dwight, the man who had refused to take arms against his country, England, and King George in the name of freedom. Instead, Major Dwight, the Tory, had run away, going south to avoid the glances of the townspeople, and he had paid with his life—yes indeed—but he'd left a family behind, a large one, and its was time to demonstrate what happened to people who had the audacity to approach the question of possible independence as a matter of simple debate.

Half a dozen men were swinging scythes in the four rectangular fields where the Dwight's grew their corn. They were singing, as if they were engaged in some recreational activity, their faces sweaty and proud with each stalk that tumbled and fell to the ground.

Smoke poured from the barn and filled the air, and still

the men kept singing.

The pigs, the flames, the screams of Madam Dwight, the absurd singing—these sights and sounds settled into Theodore's brain as burning tears ran down his cheeks. He was on his knees now, trying to find the strength to pull himself up, his mind reeling.

His older brother, Erastus, ran from the back of the home and grabbed an axe from the woodpile stacked behind the kitchen. "Damn all of you!" he shouted. "Damn each and every one of you bastards!"

He was running toward the pig pen, but one of the raiding party simply stuck his leg out, and Erastus tripped over the man's leather boot, rolling into the dirt, all the while shouting "damn you, damn you to hell!"

The two men who had set the barn ablaze were laying axes to the saplings planted along the side of the house—apple trees and a baby oak.

Theodore was on his feet now, moving slowly, stumbling toward his family—his mother and brothers and sisters, all of them shrieking and standing together as the farm was desecrated.

His sister held his little brother, Cecil, only two. His crying was audible above the singing of the men and the roar of the blaze.

The men had finished sacking the farm, but they weren't done with the family, not yet. They stood in a circle around Mrs. Dwight. Off to the side, Erastus was curled into a tight ball. The edge of the ax he had been carrying when he fell had opened up a gash on his forearm.

Theodore broke into a run and threw himself at the

nearest marauder, trying desperately to break through the ring they had formed around his mother. The man turned—a scar ran down his face, from the corner of his eye to the edge of his mouth. He seemed amused at Theodore's last minute bravery. He opened his eyes wide and spat at Theodore before pushing the heel of his hand against the boy's forehead, sending him sprawling backwards in the dirt. "Get away, little man!" he shouted.

"Nothing personal, Mrs. Dwight," declared one of the younger men, bowing with mock civility, "but there can be no ambivalence in certain matters pertaining to the welfare of these territories. I do hope you understand."

The brutish men retreated slowly, casting glances backwards as they made their way up the road, away from the ravaged Dwight farm. They continued their mindless, idiotic singing, stumbling from their exertions, belly-laughing at the scene they were leaving behind.

Theodore Dwight looked up from the ground, glancing from his mother to the departing men. "There can be no ambivalence" one of the men had said. The words echoed in Theodore's mind again and again. "No ambivalence."

His mother collapsed.

Cecil continued to scream as billows of smoke drifted across Theodore's field of vision, erasing the entire scene, which became a brown, ugly, choking memory that would stay with him for the rest of his life.

*   *   *

Night.

Theodore sat on his porch, watching Erastus running mindlessly through the yard, throwing buckets of water on the barn which was now no more than a blackened frame glowing eerily red in the glow of ten thousand sparks, dancing like fireflies as they whirled through the air each time another length of pine fell over into the ashes scattered on the ground. Erastus, seventeen, was the kind of individual who was always determined to do something in the face of adversity. He was much like Theodore's older brother Timothy: a pillar of resolution.

As for Theodore, he had cried his last tear many hours ago. He was angry now, and his resentment swirled within his breast.

Resentment?

No, more than that. Hatred—that's what he felt. Hatred for the people who had ransacked his family's farm. Perhaps they had been motivated by their misguided, unfocused belief in independence. It was more than likely, however, that they were motivated by petty jealousy against Major Timothy Dwight for being more affluent than most of Northampton's citizens.

More than anyone, Theodore now hated his father, or at least the memory of his father. Yes, Major Timothy Dwight had been a brave and successful man, but he had left his family.

He left us, Theodore thought. *He actually left us, thinking that he would increase his fortune even more. He left us, knowing of the town's growing resentment for his loyalist sentiments. He left us to endure humiliation. He left his home.*

He left me.

Theodore looked up at the night sky, hung heavy with

black rain clouds. Was God really somewhere in the firmament? If so, had he witnessed what had happened today on a little plot of land in Massachusetts?

Theodore had no earthly father, and on this June night lit only by the remnants of fire and destruction, he decided that his heavenly Father—the great and mighty God spoken of by his grandfather, Jonathan Edwards—had also deserted him.

The door behind the boy opened quietly. Mrs. Dwight stepped forward and placed a letter in Theodore's hands. "Tell Erastus to post this letter to Stratford. Your brother Timothy must be notified of what has happened here today." She spoke in a measured, even tone, and there was no expression whatsoever on her face. "It's time that he came home."

Mary Dwight turned and went inside. She had nothing else to say, no words of comfort for Theodore or Erastus. She moved slowly and deliberately, as if under a spell.

Theodore stood and brought the letter to Erastus.

Cecil's cries persisted and were drowned out only by the close, deep rumble of thunder.

An hour later, the heavens opened and the smoldering barn hissed as rain fell on its charred remains.

"Too late, Lord," Theodore mumbled while standing in the dooryard. "Too late."

He remained motionless for half an hour as the driving rain tried in vain to wash away the memories of this long day in August, 1777.

Indeed, by 1777 colonial America began to change in a fundamental way; the revolution would put into motion

change that would last generations. The seeds of this change had been planted decades earlier by Enlightenment ideas from France, Opposition thinkers from Britain and Lockean ideas regarding the individual and government. The abundance of land brought independence of mind and spirit and gave many colonists a peculiar sense of autonomy. When Britain decided to tax the colonies more after the French and Indian war in 1763, it was like cracking an egg; expecting a helpless chick, but getting a poisonous viper. The deference that marked British colonial society would begin to crumble. As the revolutionary spirit spread through many parts of the colonies, no longer were workers and artisans deferential to people like Major Dwight. In fact, pent-up resentments sometimes found an outlet (Gordon Wood). Since Major Dwight was an official of the Crown, a local magistrate and judge, he had virtually no option but to remain loyal to the King. Every facet of colonial society began to unravel, including the piety that marked much of New England.

Theodore Dwight's maternal grandfather was the great Jonathan Edwards, a leader of the first Great Awakening. He challenged the religious orthodoxy of the Puritan establishment in western Massachusetts. Edwards argued that it was not enough for people simply to come to church. Instead, they must feel God's wrath as well as his love; only a "great change of heart" could redeem a sinful person. For a while he had many followers, but in-time his power and influence waned and he was eventually banished from his own congregation in Northampton. Nevertheless, Jonathan Edwards left an indelible mark on the American religious landscape. In reaction to her father's banishment, his daughter, Mary, Theodore Dwight's mother, would never enter the body of the Northampton Congregational church again. Thus, Theodore and his siblings spent Sundays in the drafty foyer of the church. God and religion were not sources of light for Dwight at this point.

No father. No God. Theodore Dwight was rudderless as the Revolutionary storm hit.

Chapter Two

Erastus Dwight walked toward town the next morning, his left arm wrapped in a linen bandage to protect the cut on his arm. It was not a serious wound, but it ached considerably.

The ground was damp, but the storm of the previous night had continued to sail inland, and the sun was already drying out the road that Erastus traveled. He was a hearty individual, with broad shoulders and a square jaw and thick curls of black hair stopping just short of a prominent brow. He was a serious young man who had returned from his sophomore year at Yale at the news that his father's expedition to claim new lands had failed. The Spaniards, it was rumored, had killed his father's party and seized the title papers to the territories his father had intended to claim. With the damage done to his family's farm the previous day, he doubted if he would ever be able to resume his studies. His mother adamantly wished him to follow in the footsteps of his brother Timothy. She had pushed Timothy hard—indeed, she was a taskmaster with *all* of her children when it came to their education.

Sometimes Erastus thought she pushed entirely *too* hard, but that was her personality: stern and pious and dutiful.

He walked the streets of Northampton, carrying his mother's letter to Timothy. He had no doubt that his older brother would return from Stratford and, with his usual efficiency, take charge of the family's business matters. His mother, of course, would continue to be the moral imperative behind the actions of her children. That was a given.

Erastus' pace quickened as he strode past the blacksmith shop, the ringing of the anvil mingling with the sound of wagon wheels and the chatter of pedestrians on the streets of Northampton. It was a pleasant enough morning, sunny, and the scenes of normal commerce and conversation formed an odd contrast to the surreal scenes he had witnessed the previous evening. How many of these fine, upstanding citizens, he wondered, had knowledge of what had transpired at the Dwight homestead? Was he being paranoid—were people looking past him as they thought of the chores they must perform on this summer's day—or were they staring directly at him, thinking of his strong British sympathies, which in some ways were even stronger than those his father had harbored?

Past the tannery and the stationer's shop. Past the taverns, shut tight as the owners brushed the hard-packed dirt street with brooms in front of their establishments. These men, above all others, seemed to take notice of his passing—men accustomed to listening to long-winded tales and gossip as their patrons sat and smoked, their tongues growing loose from ale and whiskey.

Three dogs were herding pigs through the street just ahead. Erastus made his way through the animals and found Docket & Sons, Cobblers. Thomas Docket handled the town's posts as well as mending shoes. The couriers stopped at his shop every other day, sometimes more frequently when there were stirrings among the colonies, rumors to be confirmed or denied on the issues of oppression or liberty, loyalty or patriotism.

Erastus entered the shop, and the gaffers sitting in straight-back chairs along the wall fell silent. An old man in a corner spat his tobacco juice on the floor and coughed. Erastus dropped his mother's letter on the counter. "I'd like to post this with the next messenger," he said.

Thomas Docket, a leather apron covering most of his large, barrel-shaped chest, looked blankly at the young man who stood before him. "Got some important news, do you?"

"What's in the letter is no one's concern," Erastus said, his voice low and guarded.

Docket smiled. "Maybe news about how things are going out on the farm?"

Two of the men on the right laughed, clearing their throats when Erastus turned toward them.

"Will you post the letter, sir?" asked Erastus, turning back to Docket.

Docket held out his palm, his eyebrows raised. Erastus dropped three coins into the man's open hand. Docket's hand remained motionless. Erastus dropped another coin into the cobbler's hand . . . and then another.

"The courier will be along, I suppose," Docket remarked casually. "Maybe today. Maybe tomorrow."

"Tell me, Dwight—just how do you sleep at night?"

Erastus wheeled around to see a man staring directly into his face, a man with a scar running down his cheek. It was Alexander Barlow, one of the town's many printers. He wore a dusty, black, broad-tailed coat.

"I sleep tolerably well, thank you, sir," answered

Erastus.

Alexander Barlow had been at the farm the previous day. Erastus hadn't gotten a good look at the men through the smoke or the air tormented with waves of heat, but he was almost certain that Barlow had been there. Somewhere in the confusion, a man with a scar cutting sharply into his cheek had cris-crossed the farm several times.

"The problem," said Barlow, "is that many of us these days *don't* sleep too well, knowing that there are some folks around—some of them pretty important—who like to play things safe."

Erastus was angry, but he'd been taught, through his mother's example as much as anything else, to contain his emotions. "If you'll pardon me," he said, attempting to step around Barlow.

"No, I won't pardon you, laddie. You see this scar on my cheek? It's rather hard to miss, wouldn't you say?"

Erastus stared at Barlow, whose head was inches from his own face.

"I got this little beauty because I was working by the window in my shop on a December afternoon a few years ago. The light from candles isn't enough to set type in the winter, laddie, and it gets mighty damned chilly sitting next to the window when a cold draft seeps in, freezing your hands so you can hardly lay out a single sentence without dropping most of the letters on the floor. But it's work, laddie—it's honest work. A British soldier didn't see it that way, though, when he threw open my door on that December day and accused me of printing up pamphlets blaming his garrison for ungentlemanly conduct toward young ladies of the town."

Barlow's face was growing red, the veins showing the tension in his neck and temples. Still, Erastus said nothing.

"The bastard toppled my press, broke my windows, and ran his bayonet up the side of my face. And do you know what I was printing, young Master Dwight? Advertisements for a Christmas party! For Christmas, Master Dwight. And for that, I now must wear this handsome red scar for the rest of my life."

Barlow pushed Dwight in the chest, sending his body against Docket's counter.

"And I'll tell you this, "Barlow continued. "I print lots of pamphlets about the British these days, just like the other printers in this town do. And I'll continue to print anything that paints the lousy red-breasted bastards in a bad light."

Erastus clenched his fists, his breath coming in hard, fast, angry bursts. Slowly, he raised his right arm. The gaffers along the wall were motionless, their bodies inclined slightly in the anticipation of a brawl.

Barlow leered at Erastus, grinning malevolently, hoping the youth would swing wildly at him.

But Erastus' left arm was throbbing with pain. This wasn't the time or the place for a fight. Plus, his family needed him. It wouldn't do for him to limp home, his clothes bloody and torn. His mother would be most displeased.

There might come another day, however, when he wouldn't let his restraint carry the day. There might come a time when Alexander Barlow would be made to understand that the Dwight family had never sought to interfere with the cause of colonial independence. And Barlow would also learn that there was such a thing as showing the proper respect for the nation which had given them all life. He would learn that loyalty to a code of behavior was just as important as the patriotism sweeping up and down the coast. Men like his father had shaped the land, men whose authority derived from the king's charter to tame the coast and make it habitable for loyal British subjects. Without such loyalty, men like Barlow would not be residing in Northampton, free to pursue their trades.

Erastus walked from the village, his cheeks still red with emotion.

He left the town and walked down the lonely road to the farm that Barlow had helped throw into chaos.

CHAPTER THREE

Theodore lifted one charred plank after another, attempting to clear away the remnants of the barn. Despite the rain, some of the boards were still warm. His hands were black and bleeding.

Worse, his mother had instructed him to direct his brothers and sisters in cleaning up the farm and restoring as much order to the land as possible. But his siblings had little interest in the activity. The previous evening had been a bad dream, part of a nightmare brought by the thunderstorm. Innocence still shielded their eyes and their minds to some degree, and Theodore reckoned that such a frame of mind was not altogether bad. He loved his family, and the fact that he was faced with so much responsibility since his father's departure meant that the younger Dwights were often spared some of the sharper pains of life.

Erastus had gone into town, and the salvage operation was rapidly falling apart. Theodore decided to sneak into the woods for the next hour, maybe two. His mother would not miss him. She was tending to Cecil, who seemed to be the most traumatized by the actions of the townsmen. The smoke and the fire and the screams had, quite expectedly, left their mark on his impressionable two year old mind. Theodore would take some time for himself, perhaps rinsing his hands in the cool waters of the nearby creek.

Standing in the middle of tall sycamores, Theodore instantly felt his breathing become slower, deeper. The ground was spongy, so he removed his worn leather shoes. Better to go barefoot than to damage the leather further. There was little money to buy food, let alone new shoes.

He crept deeper into the forest sanctuary, and as he did so, a soft whistle floated on the summer air above the lush ferns. It sounded like the call of a bird, but Theodore knew that the sound came from a human, not an animal. He whistled back, though his own call was a pathetic imitation of the original.

"These are hard times, are they not, Sapling?"

"Quinno?"

"Who else would it be?"

Quinno—short for Quinnehoag—was a member of the Nipmuc, one of the dozens of local tribes that had once been members of the mighty Pequot Confederacy. Quinno was fifteen, one of only two hundred members of the Nipmuc who had managed to survive the diseases brought to the continent by Europeans during the past two hundred years. The Nipmuc—an Algonquin word for "fresh water people"—were peaceful people and blended into the countryside so well that they were virtually invisible. Quinno's father, as well as other male tribe members, did odd jobs for some of the citizens of Northampton, which is how Quinno himself had managed to learn English.

The Nipmuc were a proud people, and Theodore wondered how the people in town could not recognize how demeaning it was to ask the members of a once-great nation to haul wood or mend leather saddles or perform other menial chores. The Nipmuc and their brother tribes had lived in the forest for centuries, were a *part* of the forest, and knew the land in ways that no Massachusetts settler ever could. Should they be expected to shoulder burdens in exchange for a little corn meal?

"Your home is not the same today as it was yesterday," stated Quinno.

"No," Theodore replied. "It is not."

Quinno was silent for a moment, and then jumped down from his perch in a sugar maple.

"So what will you do now?"

"I don't know. Survive as best as I can."

"No. What will you *do*?"

Theodore stared at his friend for several seconds before realizing what he was asking. Quinno was not inquiring about Theodore's future—he was interested in what Theodore was going to do right then and there, for such was the Nipmuc mentality: one reacted to an event with an immediate action, not endless brooding on an indefinite future.

"I don't know, Quinno. What *should* I do?"

"Follow."

Dwight followed Quinno even deeper into the woods for another hundred yards, pausing only once to rinse his sore hands in the chilly waters of the Missonog, the Nipmuc name for the creek which had clear, sweet water that sang for miles as it threaded the forest brush near Northampton.

Quinno dropped to his knees and motioned silence. Theodore heard nothing, but Quinno's far keener ears had detected something in the brush up ahead. For ten minutes they lay still, bellies against the soil, making no sound whatsoever.

And then the Sapling knew why they had paused, knew why Quinno had soundlessly notched an arrow in his bow and pulled back the string with care and precision and, above all, concentration. A reddish-brown blur was visible several yards away. A deer.

Theodore wanted no part in this. The men of the town were hunters, just as his father had been, but Major Dwight had not taught Theodore the art of hunting before leaving on his ill-fated adventure, and that had always been fine by Theodore. His reverence for the forest did not include the slaughter of animals. Even now, he wanted to reach up and grab Quinno's arm so that the arrow, poised and armed with the tension of the bowstring, would sail high and miss its mark. But he dared not do such a thing, for while Quinno was his friend, he was also a Nipmuc brave who had been schooled in such skills. To be a brave was to be a hunter, and killing an animal was simply part of a larger rhythm which the tribe adhered to.

The arrow whistled through the air, attended by a split-second rustle of leaves. Theodore's eyes were shut tightly.

"Now," Quinno said, tapping Theodore on the shoulder.

The two boys advanced, the Sapling trailing timidly behind his companion.

The animal was not dead—not yet.

Quinno offered Theodore a knife. "Finish quickly," he urged.

"No," said the Sapling, turning, trying not to retch. He held the knife, and slowly, after a minute passed, Theodore took its handle. The animal was suffering. He couldn't let this go on any longer.

This is what Quinno had had in mind for Theodore the entire time. This is what his friend needed to do—right now.

Theodore ended the deer's life quickly.

He was no longer paralyzed by the fear of the day before.

CHAPTER FOUR

It had only been a week since the farm had been invaded by Alexander Barlow and his confederates, but even now, Mrs. Dwight insisted that her family honor the Sabbath. Only Cecil, who was having recurrent nightmares of the tragedy, was allowed to stay home, supervised by an older sister.

Theodore sat with his family in the vestibule of the Congregational church which sat on a well-manicured edge of Northampton. For some years now Theodore had not relished attending church services. His mother shunned the body of the church which had rejected the fervor of her father, the great Jonathon Edwards, a preacher of thunderous orations which had caused the Great Awakening to sweep through Christian souls in New England.

The Great Awakening. True piety and fervor. Respect for God the Father Almighty. Holiness—above all holiness—before partaking of the Eucharist. It was necessary that each communicant practice the necessary virtues of faith before receiving the Body of Christ.

The reputation of Theodore's grandfather had inspired awe in the youngster, sometimes fear, but always admiration. After being dismissed from the church, Edwards had become a missionary to the Indians. He was a man of faith and discipline, and that same discipline had been passed to his daughter as well as to her children, including Timothy, Erastus, and Theodore.

Yes, he admired the memory of his grandfather. If his grandfather *had* been present on this particular Sunday morning, Theodore might have needed to turn his head in shame since he felt abandoned by God. His father had been killed, and now his home had been violated. His family was looked down upon by the town, and his own mother distanced herself from other worshipers in a religion that supposedly stressed love and brotherhood and forgiveness.

Theodore was at church for his mother and no one else.

Erastus sat next to him, nervously wringing his hands, sighing heavily every few minutes.

"Be ye perfect," warned a voice from the invisible pulpit. "Be ye perfect, just as your Father in heaven is perfect."

What did it mean to be perfect, Theodore wondered. It didn't entail pillaging, and yet Alexander Barlow and his companions were sitting in the nave of the church, looking quiet and respectable.

Perfection was the forest and the elegant speech of the Missonog as it wandered through deep shadow or spectacular sunlight. It was the way Quinno padded through the underbrush. Perfection was doing what one had to do, like ending the misery of the deer. Perfection was . . .

Abigail Thorne turned her head slightly, and Theodore knew that it was just the precursor to other movements she would soon make. She always began with short gazes to her left and right. Sometimes she scratched her shoulder or swept her hand—her beautiful, white, delicate hand—along her arm as if brushing away some bit of dust. In time, she would turn her head farther, until that time when her eyes would briefly find Theodore sitting in the vestibule, outlined against the doorway which led to the sunny churchyard.

Yes, Abigail Thorne was perfection, sitting in her cinched blue dress. Theodore had watched her enter the church that morning, had seen how her breasts filled out the top of the dress. No amount of fabric could conceal her budding femininity. Her long brown hair, lustrous and fine as silk, hung down below the top of the pew behind her.

Her head was moving, turning, turning completely around—no scratching or hesitating—and her eyes fell on Theodore, and for a split second, he thought she smiled, but that had to have been his imagination, just *had* to have been, because this was church, and she dare not divert her attention from the preacher.

And it most surely had to be his imagination because he could not possibly be lucky enough to merit the overt attention of such a lovely creature, two years his senior, a creature both graceful and sensuous.

What should he do?

Something, nothing, everything.

His mind reeled, and there!—she turned again, though not all the way around this time. Perhaps she wanted to gauge his response. Or perhaps she was simply taken with him, and if that was the case . . . .

". . . As your heavenly Father is perfect," droned the voice at the front of the congregation. "For I tell you, I have not come to do away with one iota of the Law and the prophets."

Erastus was growing more agitated by the moment. He suddenly rose from his chair and left the church. His mother shot a stern look in his direction, and Theodore knew as surely as the sun would set that evening that his mother would take Erastus into a room of their home and demand an explanation for his unexpected departure.

But the legs of Erastus' chair had also grated against the floorboards, causing Abigail to turn yet again, this time all the way around, and look at Theodore since a noise was a perfectly understandable distraction. And yes, the corners of her mouth were spread in the slightest of smiles—a smile so faint that no one could ever have detected it if not actively looking for it, expecting it.

That smile was perfection.

The admonitions of his grandfather Jonathan crumbled into dust—the warnings of damnation, the interminable commandments and inner purification, the examinations of one's conscience—it all crumbled beneath the ethereal glance of this flower and a smile which certainly held a message, one that would be deciphered at length when he had time to be alone, in his room or in the forest.

He had been forgotten by God, but noticed by Abigail Throne. For Theodore Dwight, such a trade-off was perfectly acceptable on an August Sunday morning.

Theodore was having a very great awakening.

Chapter Five

Mrs. Dwight had a different type of awakening in mind for Theodore: study, punctuated by chores, from sunrise to sunset.

Timothy would be arriving home within the month, after the affairs of his household in Stratford were put in order. His wife had just given birth to a son, plus Timothy was tutoring several children and occasionally preaching at local churches, having been an outstanding theology student at Yale.

As for Erastus, he still did much of the manual labor around the farm, but he was growing increasingly distracted. Even the admonitions of his mother had not been enough to cure his growing moodiness. When he performed his daily tasks, he frequently talked to himself. He seemed sullen and withdrawn. Often he leaned against the split-rail fence bordering the eastern boundary of the farm and stared off in the distance.

Theodore was expected to pick up the slack, to chop wood, feed the two remaining hogs, tend the vegetable garden, and keep his brothers and sisters in line . . .

. . . And study. Always there was more study, more reading and memorization. During the morning hours, he was expected to commit long scriptural passages to memory. It was dull and boring. Theodore didn't really appreciate the necessity of learning the hundreds of Jewish laws and rites of purification contained in the books of Leviticus and Deuteronomy. The air was hot in the room his father had used as a study. There was no circulation whatsoever since Madam Dwight did not allow any open doors or windows in the home lest dust accumulate on the floors. And if she entered the room and found Theodore's mind wandering, his gaze focused on a green rise out back, Theodore was forced to listen to a ten minute lecture on following in the scholarly footsteps of his brother Timothy. His mother's voice was harsh, shrill, and full of reprimand.

But why should *he* get such a scolding? He, Theodore, had not abandoned his family in order to go to West Florida. And he was not responsible for the ransacking of the farm or the erratic behavior of Erastus or the increasing silence and immobility of Cecil.

Theodore was growing into a strong young man, physically imposing, with muscular arms and broad shoulders, and yet he did not think it fair that his mother place so many of the family's burdens upon those very shoulders. He would be glad when Timothy finally arrived home again.

Looking out the window, his eye fell yet again on the green mound behind the home. Its curve was gentle, subtle, not unlike the curve he beheld in the silhouette of Abigail Thorne.

The door behind him opened quickly and then slammed shut.

"Theodore Dwight." A commanding tone of voice. His mother's.

The rustle of a skirt approaching. He dare not turn around—only sit up straight and listen.

"Straighter! Sit up straighter, Theodore."

He pushed his back firmly against the uncomfortable wooden back of his chair.

And then his mother's index finger was firmly tapping the pages of the open bible on the oak desk.

"This is the Song of Songs," Mrs. Dwight said. "That book is not to be read in this home."

She leaned over and grasped the book and tore a handful of pages from the Bible. Theodore still could not see the imposing figure of his mother, for he dare not turn to look at her lest he be labeled as disobedient or confrontational.

And then she was gone, the door having slammed shut, causing the only breeze in the study that morning, a slight whisper of air which sent the papers on the desk fluttering to the floor.

Theodore let out a barely perceptible sigh. The only passages he had actually committed to memory for the past three days had come from the Song of Songs. It was pure poetry, liquid and alive.

Your love is more delightful than wine;
    delicate is the fragrance of your perfume,
    your name is an oil poured out . . .

Or . . .

    You ravish my heart,
    my sister, my promised bride,
    you ravish my heart
    with a single one of your glances,
    with one pearl of your necklace.

And . . .

> *Your navel is a bowl well rounded*
> *with no lack of wine,*
> *your belly a heap of wheat*
>
> *surrounded with lilies.*
> *Your two breasts are two fawns,*
> *twins of a gazelle.*
> *Your neck is an ivory tower . . .*

His grandfather Jonathan Edwards had never preached on this book of the Bible, full of longing and sensuality.

Reluctantly, Theodore picked up several books—seventeenth century textbooks—and papers strewn at his feet. There was Roger Cawdry's *Table Alphabeticall of Hard Words* and John Bullock's *English Expositor* and Blount's *Glossographia*. Every book was dry as dust and dead as bone. Essays, maps, and prayer books. Boring. And the dictionaries—little more than spelling tables—usually illustrated their words with more passages from scripture. "C" for Commandment. "S" for Sin. "V" for virtue.

And "B" for boring, thought Theodore.

The light outside dimmed as clouds rolled in, obscuring the golden haze hanging outside of the window. A few distant rumbles stirred the sky off in the distance.

And then there was a bright flash and a loud thunder-crack which shook the house.

"No, merciful God!" shrieked Mrs. Dwight from the other side of the house.

There was more thunder, the sky nearly black while rain pelted the clapboards of the Dwight home.

Footsteps hurried through the hall outside of the study.

"No!" cried Mrs. Dwight, running to her room. "No, no, no!"

This was the second time in less than a week that Theodore's mother had run to her bedroom during a thunderstorm, burying her head beneath the covers and crying to God the Father for mercy. She had always been a little skittish when it came to bad weather, gathering her brood from the yard in order to protect them, but ever since the evening when the farm had been violated by her fellow townspeople, the crashing of thunder caused her severe panic. She would scream, wide-eyed, pleading with God to spare her family further degradation.

Theodore looked out the window and saw Erastus standing in the downpour, his form etched by the silver lightning every few seconds. He was standing immobile, unfazed by the torrents slapping his body.

Mary Dwight was wailing even louder now in her bedroom down the hall.

Theodore calmly closed the family Bible and neatly stacked the other books on the edge of the desk. He rose from his chair, walked to the corner of the study, and slumped to the floor.

There he cried. His family life was utterly chaotic.

Chapter Six

The thunderstorm had passed, and his mother had emerged from the gloom of her bedroom, managing the household during the afternoon hours as if nothing whatsoever had happened, as if her children should keep no thought in their puzzled minds of their mother locking herself away from the rain. She had supervised her daughters in the cleaning of cast iron pots and the sweeping of the floors. She was terribly concerned that the storm might have blown dust beneath the cracks of the doors, and she simply would not abide any disorder around her house.

The day had passed slowly, and the family had eaten a meager meal of boiled potatoes and corn bread in relative silence shortly after sunset. There was nothing, really, to be said.

Mary Dwight retired early. This was always a welcome occurrence to Theodore, those nights when his mother retreated to the safety of her bedroom once again. When her door was closed after dark, he knew that she would not appear until the next morning. His sisters would finish straightening the house and put Cecil to bed.

It was Cecil who now wandered by the open doorway of Theodore's second floor room.

"Come in," Theodore urged his younger brother.

Cecil shook his head. He spoke little these days.

Theodore patted his lap. "Come on," he persisted. "Don't be afraid."

Cecil toddled forth tentatively. His eyes were bright and large and blue, but they were also filled with a certain degree of trepidation. Theodore picked him up and placed him on his knees.

"How about a horsy ride? Would you like a horsy ride?"

Cecil nodded his head slowly.

Theodore's legs bounced up and down, shaking his little brother in a mock gallop across an imagined meadow. "It's rather bumpy tonight, isn't it?" said Theodore, his hands on Cecil's waist. He dipped the child slightly to the left and then the right. "Yes, quite bumpy, but we're riding to meet our older brother Timothy, who will be home soon. Do you remember your brother Timothy?"

Cecil shrugged his shoulders.

"Well, that's okay, because he'll be home soon, and you and he will get along quite well."

Cecil made no reply.

"But for now," Theodore said, "I think the road is going to get even bumpier—yes indeed!" His knees moved up and down faster and faster until Cecil, unable to help himself, began to giggle and beg for more.

"More horsy! More horsy!"

Theodore and Cecil rode for another half hour until Theodore's legs felt numb. But the youngster had had a good time before his sister took him off to bed.

"Bye," said Cecil timidly, waving.

Theodore winked.

CHAPTER SEVEN

Theodore held a book in his hands—*the* book, the most important and interesting book he had ever read: *Clarissa* by Samuel Richardson. Actually, the book, extremely long, existed in several different volumes, and Theodore only possessed five of the eight, these having been found outside the preacher's home, lying on top of a fence post last June. Theodore had snatched them away, although he certainly could have found some of the volumes in many other places in Northampton. It was the town's secret vice, harboring these books, much of it written in the form of correspondence. It was another sign that freethinking was more acceptable these days. Thoughts of liberty went hand in hand now with religious toleration and a certain acceptance or more relaxed morals. It was an age of enlightenment, when people could think on things once forbidden by the strict, collective puritanical mind of New England. Of course, if Theodore's mother found the books in her home, which Dwight hid under his mattress ticking, there would be hellfire and damnation in the Dwight homestead.

The book was about sex more than anything else, at least to Theodore's way of thinking. He had not bothered to read every page in his possession, for some parts of the book were far more interesting than others. The most important passages had been marked with folded page corners, these pages being read and reread almost nightly by the light from the two candles on Theodore's night stand

The lovely young Clarissa was to be married to a wealthy man she detested. Clarissa rejected the union. Her family locked her away, hoping she would come to her senses. But there was a dashing man—Lovelace was his name—who pretended to be Clarissa's savior. He would mend her strained relations with her family.

But what he *actually* did was take her to London and find her lodging at a brothel, where he began to grow increasingly fond of Clarissa.

A brothel. The very concept of such a place astounded the midnight imagination of Theodore Dwight. It was a place where love was *sold*, and here was innocent young Clarissa, living amidst the whores—what a fascinating word that was too—being courted by the rakish Lovelace.

In letter after letter, Clarissa was puzzled as how to react, but react she did, flirting shamelessly with Lovelace, urging him on, becoming the consummate coquette, the moth making love to the flame again and again, contemplating the warmth of a thousand pleasures while ruin lies just inches away.

Letter after letter, page after page. Theodore was mesmerized. The world was so much larger than Northampton, so much more sophisticated in its thinking. And accepting—yes, accepting of so many diverse behaviors, behaviors long forbidden by the black frocks and white collars that had spoken in grave tones of piety in small, plain meeting houses during harsh New England winters.

Was reading *Clarissa* sinful? Theodore supposed it still might be considered such by most people, at least outwardly, but Theodore could see that men and women were more daring. They exchanged glances, they talked, and they touched. And if one had a sharp eye and was alert, one could see them behind buildings, holding each other, kissing each other on the lips or the neck or . . .

Theodore was a moth, sitting nightly by his two candles, pouring over every word on every page that he had marked. Clarissa was always leading Lovelace on and then backing away—wanting him, fascinated by his manner, his words and his body.

Did women really act this way? Was it possible?

"Abigail," Theodore whispered into the still air of his room, watched only by the shadows on his wall, and if those shadows were good or evil, he cared not the slightest bit, for his mind was swimming with thoughts of . . .

"Abigail . . . Abigail my dearest—"

Had he actually uttered that word: *dearest*?

He closed his eye in order to better see Abigail Thorn turning around in church. But just as quickly, his mind plucked her from the dreary surroundings of church and placed her on the gentle green slope behind his home. Suddenly, the month was April, and the cinch around the middle of her blue waist was in his hands. And then her own arms slipped past his, wrapping around his back and drawing him closer so that she could rest her lips against his neck and whisper "Theodore."

"This is sinful," his mother whispered, her form a mere shadow flickering on the wall.

"No," said another shadow. "It is glorious and wonderful."

It was Clarissa herself speaking these words, speaking them especially for Theodore. "Kiss her, and properly."

Theodore looked into the sultry eyes of Abigail Thorne and kissed her on the mouth.

She was quite accepting of Theodore's gift.

"Yes," whispered the shadows dancing along the wall. "Yes."

His mother's whisper was gone.

This was joyous . . . and also maddening.

He must *do* something—anything—to release his energy, for he felt almost as if he suffered from a fever, his brow hot, his palms sweaty, his pulse racing like a fawn through the woods.

Fawns, yes. *Your two breasts are fawns . . . your neck is an ivory tower. . .*

His mother had ripped the Song of Songs from the Bible, but the words were already a part of his heat-tempered brain.

Theodore got out the rough parchment and the quill beneath his bed. He would write a letter, express his love. Yes, he would write a letter, just as in *Clarissa.* It was the proper way to reveal his sentiments. His hands moved quickly, trembling as they cleared a space on his night stand.

How to begin?

My Dearest Abigail . . .

Yes, of course, how else?

But what came next?

"Tell her what you feel in your heart," whispered Clarissa, her voice as smooth as silk. "Don't be timid."

"But—"

"But you *must*," said the enticing shadow, or you shall

never get a wink of sleep this night."

"But I have never even spoken with Abigail," Theodore protested.

"Until tonight," reassured Clarissa. "Until tonight."

My Dearest Abigail,
I think of you this night, and only you. And if I could have just one prayer answered in all the world, it would be that you allow your hand to rest in mine for some small period of time.
Your humble servant,
Theodore

"This is ridiculous," said Theodore, reading back the brief opening of his heart. "It is hopeless."

"It is a beginning," comforted the shadowy presence of Clarissa. "Those sentences touch my heart."

Theodore smiled.

The dark shapes on his wall were shadows—only shadows.

But he was content. He placed the writing materials beneath his bed as far as he could reach, up against the wall. He then held his letter to Abigail over the candles' flames until it was nothing but a few black ashes which had seconds before represented the entire range and depth of his feelings. That particular letter would never be sent.

But there might be others in the future.

"A" is for Abigail, he thought.

He blew out the candle and fell asleep. His dreams had never been more satisfying. They danced through his sleeping brain, cousins of the sinewy shapes that had graced his wall earlier in the evening.

CHAPTER EIGHT

There was only one person whom Theodore was willing to confide in, especially when it pertained to personal matters of the heart—or physical longings best understood by someone his own age, someone definitely outside of his immediate family.

Quinno listened to the tale of lovely Abigail and her sly flirtations with Theodore during church services. But Quinno was perceptive, and he heard more in the Sapling's voice than the young boy was actually confessing. He was aware of the desires his younger companion was describing and how those desires coursed through a young man's bloodstream with each heartbeat.

Young Quinno was familiar with lust, in fact, since the Nipmuc were unashamed of their own sexual urges.

"Come with me, Sapling," advised Quinno, jerking his head, his eyes dancing with mischief. "There is something you should see."

Theodore, as always, followed his trusted companion into the dark shadows of the forest. Quinno was more than a mere friend: he was a guide who frequently led Theodore into the deeper mysteries of life, those things which the white man either did not understand or could not adequately explain.

Orlando's Nemesis

*   *   *

The young girls of Quinno's small village were bathing in one of the deeper areas of the Missonog. They were laughing, talking with great animation amongst themselves as they sat and splashed in the cool waters rushing past their slender bodies.

And they were quite naked.

And then the unthinkable happened. Quinno stepped from behind the dogwood where he and his friend had been hiding and walked unashamedly toward the creek. The young girls, ranging from fourteen to eighteen years of age, did not flee—indeed they did nothing at all except greet their tribal brother as he sat down a few feet from the water's edge. They conversed in Algonquin for several minutes, after which Quinno turned and motioned for Theodore to step forward.

Theodore remained motionless. No one could see him hunched beneath the branches of the dogwood, but he was blushing nonetheless.

"They won't bite," Quinno remarked with a slight laugh, "unless you really want them too."

A few days before, Theodore might have remained frozen, just as he had been during the tense moments when his farm had been pillaged. But so many things had changed in just a short time. He had killed a deer. And he had spoken with the beautiful Clarissa, after a fashion, and then poured forth his heart in writing, in black and white letters that existed in the real world and not just his imagination.

He had learned how to make decisions.

He stepped forward and stood next to the seated

Quinno.

One of the dark-skinned maidens said something to him in her native tongue. Theodore understood very few Nipmuc words, but he knew this much about the girl's communication. She was clearly pleased with his presence, fully at ease, and whatever she had said was certainly not a protest of any sort.

"She wants to know if you'll join her," Quinno volunteered.

Theodore shook his head. But his eyes remained fixed on the lovely maiden, the ends of her black hair floating in a hundred different directions in the rushing water. She had been crouching, but she suddenly stood straight up and squeezed the water from her hair. She then arched her back, causing her breasts to curve forward into the air.

Theodore could think only of the full moon as he stared at the girl's breasts, round and wet and inviting.

"Let's go," said Quinno, standing. "They might get offended if you don't take off your clothes soon and wade in."

The two boys left. Theodore could hear the maidens giggling as he walked back into the inviting gloom of the forest.

*   *   *

It was night, and Theodore knew that he should have been home hours ago. His mother would be very unhappy, to say the least. She would surely look harshly at her son with her dark brown eyes, her hair pulled back severely in a bun. And then she would scold him just as her father had scolded his congregations for their sinful behavior, for willful disobedience. She would also demand to know where he had been and what he had been doing. Why had he not done his chores or pursued his studies? And then he would lie, telling her that he had fallen asleep in the woods or lost track of time.

"Look," whispered Quinno, pointing at the silver moon which floated effortlessly above a plateau in the distance. A small shape appeared, silhouetted against the bright white light.

It was a wolf.

Quinno lifted his head; his chin pointed straight up at the night sky, and howled into the darkness. Far off, the wolf raised its own head and answered the call.

"It is your turn, Sapling. Speak to the wolf."

Theodore did not hesitate. He raised his head and sent a loud call into the chilly evening air. The wolf, however, didn't answer.

"That was terrible," Theodore admitted. "It sounded like the wheeze of a bellows at the blacksmith's shop."

"Like this," instructed Quinno, filling his lungs with the night, expelling the air in several bursts, each punctuated by a slight pause while his lips formed an oval to better channel the wild nature of his cries. Again the wolf gave response.

Theodore swallowed large gulps of air . . . and then blurted out a laugh at his own feeble attempt.

"You must inhale smoothly," counseled Quinno. "You must not be self-conscious. Become the wolf. Let the cry flow from your spirit."

Theodore inhaled slowly and steadily, closed his eyes, and sent a clear, high-pitched howl into the Massachusetts night. The wolf, still poised in front of the large oval moon, sent a long reply into the air.

Theodore felt exhilarated. He had never before vented so much energy at one time. He felt free.

And happy.

Staring at the moon, growing rounder as it rose slowly above the plateau, he recalled the breast of the maiden as it rose above the surface of the Missonog earlier that day.

The way he was feeling now, unburdened and very much alive—perhaps this was the way one felt after actually touching the smooth skin of a young woman.

Or the ivory neck of Abigail Thorne.

Theodore left the company of Quinno and headed home. He was unconcerned with the chastisement which awaited him upon crossing the threshold of the Dwight residence.

Chapter Nine

It was May of 1778, and Timothy Dwight sat at the oak desk where his father had once poured over the business ledgers and financial considerations of the Dwight family. He was an even-tempered man with a light complexion and thinning hair. He gazed from the tax notices on his desk to the green rise visible through the window and then back at the papers. Matters with his family—emotional and financial—were grave, but Timothy was a man who acted deliberately and patiently. This was not a time for panic. It was a time for leadership. His mother expected no less from him, and he would not disappoint her. He knew that while he had inherited his father's determination and endurance, he had inherited prudence and good judgment from his mother.

His task was daunting. Besides the family home, his father had left other properties in Northampton amounting to over three thousand acres. This real estate was appraised at 4,433 pounds, the personal estate being worth 134 pounds. The problem at hand was that the Massachusetts economy was absolutely deplorable. The currency had depreciated terribly, being worth only one fortieth of its face value. Collecting the money farmers owed his family was almost impossible under such circumstances, making it equally problematic to pay the family's taxes. Selling his father's lands was not really an option. With the devalued currency, any sale would yield almost no appreciable profit.

So be it. God did not give men burdens they couldn't carry. "God works for the good in all things," he reminded himself, quoting one of St. Paul's letters as he stared through the window of the study. He would work two of the farms his father had left. He was an intelligent man, well-educated, and most of all, he wasn't afraid of hard work.

He was also worried, however, about the emotional welfare of his family. Erastus was withdrawn, and Theodore, while a courteous young man, seemed more and more taken to wandering through the woods or going to bed early, sometimes reading late into the night. He was almost positive he could hear the scratching of a quill on paper behind Theodore's door. As for Cecil, he could be completely carefree—or quiet and withdrawn, like Erastus. A certain melancholy had settled over his family, much like unclean spirits had possessed people in the New Testament. It would be his duty to exorcize such sadness. His wife, cheerful and industrious, would be an enormous help.

He would also start a school in order to nurture the minds of those people which God had put in his charge. Plus he had also been offered the pulpit at nearby Westfield, a position he intended to take. He would derive income from both activities.

God had clearly called him back to his home. A lesser man might have been overwhelmed by the amount of work which lay in the future, but not Timothy Dwight. If there was a mountain to be moved, then one started chipping away at it, hauling away its rubble one bucketful at a time.

Timothy took the gospel's admonition to "Be ye perfect" very seriously.

CHAPTER TEN

Theodore did not freeze this time when he saw the men pacing leisurely up the road, holding axes and torches in their hands. Thanks to Quinno, he knew how to make a decision swiftly.

He bolted for the rear of the house, where Erastus was shucking ears of corn. "They're back," he told his brother breathlessly. "And they have—" He swallowed hard and gasped for air. "Torches." His chest heaved over and over again. "Axes, too. And guns."

"How many this time?" asked Erastus, tossing an ear of corn to the ground.

"Six. Six men in all."

"Where are—"

"Still three hundred yards away."

"What about—"

"Yes, Barlow's with me. In the lead."

Erastus disappeared inside the kitchen for fifteen seconds—no more—and emerged with a rifle. "And you?" he said, shooting a look at his younger brother.

"Yes, me!" Theodore exclaimed, scrambling after his brother, who was already in motion, already cutting across a thin patch of woods occupying the ground where the road up to the house curved gently.

"What are you going to do?" called Theodore, jumping over bushes and dodging low branches.

"Shut up!" cautioned Erastus, wheeling sharply, "before you give us away."

Theodore nodded. His pulse had never been faster. He didn't know what Erastus had planned, if anything, but Theodore wasn't going to just crouch in the shadows this time, wasn't going to see his family terrorized again. It was a matter of self-defense, a matter of survival. His family couldn't afford to lose anything else, even with Timothy back at home. *Especially* with Timothy back at home, finally earning money from his labor, his school, his preaching.

Erastus slowed. They were coming up on the road. They could hear the sound of footsteps moving over the dirt, kicking loose gravel. The voices of the men were low. They spoke in menacing tones that Theodore could hear from behind the row of pines where he and Erastus knelt.

Erastus raised the rifle and steadied the long barrel, which rested in his left hand.

Was he going to shoot Barlow, shoot all of them?

Sensing his brother's concerns, Erastus paused. "A warning shot. That's all."

Theodore's heart pounded like a hummingbird's, every nerve in his body alert.

Erastus' finger curled around the trigger. Beads of sweat popped out on his forehead. This moment, this preparing to fire, seemed to Theodore to last an eternity.

Crack!

The musket ball whizzed through the air, knocking the

wide-brimmed, shabby hat from the head of Alexander Barlow, who immediately dove for the ground.

Barlow's five compatriots turned immediately and fled. They were in the open, exposed. They weren't going to risk their lives in order to have a little fun at the Dwights' expense.

Erastus sprang through the green cover at the side of the road, hurling himself upon the prostrate body of Barlow before the man knew what was happening. His right fist crashed down into Barlow's face again and again until Barlow's blood flowed down his cheek.

Theodore stepped out into the road, his fists rolled into tight balls of anger, ready to come to his brother's aid if necessary.

"Stop!" ordered Timothy, who had heard the shot and immediately started up the road from the house.

Barlow climbed to his feet slowly, turned away . . .

. . . and then spun and threw himself at Timothy.

Theodore's mind worked at lightning speed. He wasn't afraid to use brute force, but Quinno had taught him something long ago, a way to immobilize an enemy. Theodore dove toward the ground, his arms encircling the ankles of Alexander Barlow. He hugged the man's legs tightly, and in less than ten seconds, the man broke off his attack against Timothy, falling awkwardly into the dirt.

Barlow rolled away, dazed. He wiped the blood from his mouth and cheeks and stared up at Theodore. "You'd do best not to cross me, little whelp. This is a matter between men."

"There can be no ambivalence when it comes to my family," Theodore shot back.

Barlow cocked his head at the insolence of the young man daring to challenge him.

"Go back into town," Timothy cautioned the man. "And leave this family alone. We still have friends enough in this territory to deal with the likes of you and your friends."

Barlow glared at Timothy. "I'll go, Preacher. But I'm not finished with these two little pups of yours. They best be watchful the next time they walk down a road late in the evening."

Barlow stumbled out of sight, leaving the three Dwight brothers alone.

"The next time—assuming there *is* a next time—you let me know immediately," Timothy informed his brothers sternly before walking away. He was not pleased with his siblings.

The two men walked back to their farm, keeping their distance from the disgruntled Timothy.

There can be no ambivalence, thought Theodore. He raised his head and howled into the air like a wolf.

Erastus turned toward his brother, puzzled. But he said nothing.

CHAPTER ELEVEN

The Dwight family walked home from church several weeks after Barlow's appearance at the farm. Since it was Sunday, there would be no study and few, if any, chores for the children. It was midsummer, hot and humid, and the air was hazy and oppressive. At home, however, the dining room was cool and pleasant as the family sat down to a dinner of pork, potatoes, and carrots. Timothy was being given food as payment for his duties as schoolmaster and preacher, and the daily toil on his father's farms had eased the financial burdens somewhat. On Sundays, they could afford to eat well, sometimes even enjoying a pudding or custard for desert.

If Northampton held a grudge against the Dwights, it was not in evidence in its collective demeanor toward the family. Indeed, Timothy seemed to be gaining favor rapidly in the community. Workers even sometimes argued good naturedly as to whom would be allowed to work at his side out in the fields. Despite his serious views of life, Timothy had a sunny, light disposition and treated his fellow townspeople and workers well, always listening to their comments patiently as they described their own hardships in the tough economic times they all faced.

Life was still immensely hard for Theodore, however. Timothy was always away, always busy—always, in his own words, doing the business of his heavenly Father.

And his earthly mother.

Mary Dwight was growing more erratic in her behavior. She seemed outwardly pleased that the family's burdens had eased, and even smiled in the presence of visitors or relatives. But she could also be sullen or harsh for days at a time, criticizing her children if they did not apply themselves to their studies, if they chewed their food too loudly or had a dirty fingernail after washing up.

Theodore knew it would be cooler in the forest, and ate his dinner quickly.

His mother had retired to her room after the midday meal to rest. Timothy was seated in the study, where Theodore knew he would read and doze for the remainder of the afternoon, keeping his activities to a minimum on the Sabbath. His wife would spend the afternoon hours with her child, who was becoming a constant playmate of Cecil's.

No one would notice if Theodore slipped away in the lazy hours of the long day.

He checked his appearance in one of the home's two mirrors before quietly leaving. He wanted to look his best.

*   *   *

Abigail smiled at Theodore as he approached. "I got your letter," she said, her voice a smooth whisper that seemed to Theodore to be almost indistinguishable from the music of the Missonog. "Do you really find me . . . beautiful?" Abigail blinked twice. The shadows of the forest kept her high angular cheeks in dark shadow.

"Yes," replied Theodore, stepping toward Abigail.

"I've made us a bed," she said, taking Theodore's hand. "From ferns. This way."

Abigail led Timothy to a spot surrounded by tall sycamores. They would have all the privacy they needed.

Abigail sat on the ground first, patting the lush ferns, motioning for Theodore to join her.

"Don't be shy," she said, laughing.

Theodore was fifteen now, but Abigail, who would soon be eighteen, had a certain ease and sophistication in her speech, in the way she drew Theodore toward her with the body language of a smile and an extended arm. Yes, he was indeed shy, but he was also powerless in the presence of such unparalleled beauty.

Abigail drew him down until his body rested against her own, kissing him lightly on the mouth.

Theodore kissed her back and stroked her long brown hair. She reached up, combing a leaf from the top of his head.

He looked for a long time into her eyes, the eyes he had strained so hard to see during church services. They gazed back at Theodore without a trace of shame. *This is salvation,* he thought. *This is all I desire in life.*

They lay with each other for a long time, kissing, holding each other.

But mostly they looked at each other, occasionally speaking in soft tones of the beauty of the forest.

"Perhaps we could . . . " Theodore's voice trailed off.

"Yes?"

"See each other more often so that we could . . . "

Abigail smiled. "Bundle. You want to bundle, right?"

Theodore fell silent, embarrassed. "Yes," he admitted, little more than his lips silently moving.

Abigail chose her words carefully so as not to hurt her companion's feelings. "That would, of course, be wonderful, but you are younger than I. And your mother—" She smiled faintly. "I've seen her stern looks on Sunday mornings. Our families would not allow us to share a bed together, even under supervision."

"Not even with a bundling board?" Theodore asked.

"No, not even with a board to separate us. We shall do our bundling right here."

Abigail loosened the top strings which kept her dress closed tightly beneath her throat. She then took Theodore's hand and slowly placed it beneath her fabric, on her breast.

"Will you kiss me, Theodore? Properly?"

Theodore placed his lips against Abigail's. For the next hour, he had no sense of time. If there was such a thing as home and hearth lying beyond the deep woods, he was not aware of it.

For the moment, this was his world.

*   *   *

The sky was a deep blue as Theodore meandered along the road. He was taking the long way home, for he was in no rush to have his normal existence close around him once again. He looked up occasionally, hoping to see the first star magically appear as the sky continued to darken. When he saw it, he intended to make a wish.

A wagon rumbled toward him, the horse pulling its load slowly and wearily. The driver was slumped over, his hat pulled far down over his face. It was not uncommon to see a sleeping driver at the reins on a Sunday evening.

Theodore ambled on, his thoughts of Abigail holding his imagination firmly.

The wagon was drawing even with him.

"Good Sabbath to ya, laddie!" cried Alexander Barlow from the rear of the wagon. "Need a ride, young man?"

Theodore drew in his breath, his eyes wide with alarm and surprise.

But he had no time to react. Barlow and the driver had Theodore in the back of the wagon in less than thirty seconds. A hood was placed over his head, and his hands were tied behind his back.

The wagon lurched forward, the horse's hooves striking the road hard.

"We'll see just how brave you are without your brothers around, laddie."

The voice of Alexander Barlow was filled with satisfaction.

And malice.

Chapter Twelve

When the hood was finally removed, Theodore found himself in the back room of Docket & Sons. Thomas Docket and Alexander Barlow loomed over the frightened, seated figure of Theodore Dwight. The room smelled of leather that had been rubbed with oil. Shoes and boots lined shelves and hung from nails protruding from the rough-hewn rafters. A single oil lamp provided weak light for the entire space. Theodore saw two other men, seated on pork barrels in the shadows across the room.

"What do you want?" Theodore asked. He was terrified, but he was able to keep his voice steady. He gripped the arms of the chair to prevent his hands from trembling. He was determined not to show weakness to his captors.

Barlow smiled innocently. "Just a little respect," he said, his voice as patient as a schoolmaster's while explaining a problem in arithmetic. "It's that simple."

Theodore remained silent. He wasn't sure what kind of response Barlow expected.

"We mean you no harm," said Thomas Docket, smiling. "No harm whatsoever."

"Then why was I brought here with my hands tied?" asked Theodore, looking from Docket to Barlow."

"It's like this, laddie," Barlow began. "We—"

"We just want to have a little discussion with you," interrupted Docket. "Mr. Barlow here sometimes has a tendency to get . . . rather emotional, shall we say."

The two men in the shadows laughed and shifted their positions. Theodore wondered if they were confederates of Barlow, men who had helped ransack his farm.

"We can't have members of your family shooting at people, now can we?" asked Docket.

"Erastus meant no harm," Theodore stated. "But Mr. Barlow here was up to no good the other day. He was coming back to our farm with some others. They were armed."

"That's quite a serious charge," Docket said, a frown spreading across his face. "Serious indeed."

The door to the back room flew open.

It was Erastus. He stood in the doorway, anger in his face, beads of perspiration hanging from his jaw. He breathed heavily, as if he had been running.

"Leave my brother alone," Erastus demanded. "Release him."

One of the men sitting against the far wall rose and stepped into the dim yellow light. It was the town constable.

"Mr. Barlow here says that you and your brother attacked him the other day," explained the constable.

Erastus clenched and unclenched his fists. "They ruined my family's farm, and I'm not going to allow them to do it again."

"Did they do any damage to your land the other day?" questioned the constable, his hands holding the front of his vest while resting officiously on his chest.

Erastus took a deep breath. "No. They didn't."

The constable looked down at Theodore. "And you—did you jump into the road while your brother was beating Mr. Barlow here?"

Barlow rubbed his cheeks, still red and sore from the blows Erastus had rained down on his face.

Theodore remained silent.

"That's answer enough for me," remarked the constable.

Erastus plunged forward. "If you have a quarrel with me, then it's me you should have sought out. You have no cause to detain my brother."

"I think you need to cool down a little bit, Master Dwight," said the constable. "For your own good, as well as Mr. Barlow's. Escort Master Dwight to the jail, Mr. Docket."

Barlow and Docket took Erastus by the elbows and guided him toward the door.

"What about my brother?" Erastus cried, turning around.

The constable rubbed his chin thoughtfully. "Why don't you run along home now, son," he said to the younger Dwight.

Theodore stood. "I'll be back with Timothy," he promised his brother.

Theodore left the cobbler's, his mind trying to put the events of the past hour into some kind of perspective.

He didn't like being called "son." He was fifteen now, and his stature exceeded that of most people his age.

Timothy would know what to do.

When he reached the edge of town, he broke into a run.

Orlando's Nemesis

Chapter Thirteen

Erastus sat on the bed in the basement cell of the town jail—the very jail his father had helped to build. It was the very same jail, in fact, where his father had once been detained because of his loyalties to the British crown. Was this what freedom from England meant—detention in a jail because one had tried to protect his property? Was this not an abuse of power equal to the very things which the Patriots were accusing the British of?

Erastus' nerves were frayed. He stood in his cell and paced, running his hands through his hair again and again. Barlow's actions made no sense. Timothy's presence in Northampton had been a reconciling force between his family and those who had treated the Dwights unfairly. He was looked up to, respected. He was a man of God, and many townspeople even entrusted Timothy with the care and education of their children every day.

Erastus took a deep breath. There were always men like Barlow, he realized—malcontents and troublemakers—and there always would be. It was a fact he would have to accept.

He wondered what his mother would think of his present circumstances. Would she be outraged at the treatment of her son? Would she hold the town responsible for this humiliation just as she held the Congregational church responsible for the humiliation and rejection of her father? Or would she blame *him*—Erastus—for bringing more trouble upon her family? She was so unpredictable.

*   *   *

The constable faced Erastus. He held a document in his hand. "You are charged, Mr. Dwight, with aiding and abetting the enemy," he read. "Henceforth, you will be prohibited from discharging firearms."

"I have had no dealings with the British!" cried the incensed Erastus. "What are you talking about?"

"Mr. Barlow is a Patriot," the constable informed Erastus. "An attack upon his person is an attack upon all who share his sentiments."

"That's absurd! He was trying to destroy my farm again. Do you expect my family to sit back and not defend itself?"

The constable looked sternly at Erastus. "We expect unity in our cause against the British. Everything else is secondary to that unity, including your family's welfare."

"This is unlawful!" protested Erastus. "It is outrageous, and furthermore—"

The prison door slammed shut.

The constable was clearly not interested in what Erastus had to say. The charges were perfunctory. Reasoning with the constable, Barlow, Docket—with *any* of the people who despised his family—was a waste of time.

Erastus stood by the window, which was just above

street level. The citizens of Northampton walked past, talking of mundane matters, such as the need for a new harness for a team of horses. Children ran past, rolling a barrel hoop with a hickory stick. A group of young women discussed the gentlemen they were interested in and the possibilities of talking with them at a picnic. Somewhere in the distance, a fiddler was playing a lively tune, a sharp contrast to Ersatus' grim surroundings.

And then a shadow fell across the window. Erastus moved closer to the window and squinted, trying to see past the dusty panes and the iron bars.

There was a blinding flash. A thunderous roar sent Erastus reeling back into his jail.

"Just a warning shot," said a familiar voice. "Nothing to worry about."

There was a cackle of laughter and the sound of someone running. Slowly, over a period of minutes, people gathered around the broken window, peering in, gawking at the cringing form of Erastus Dwight.

Erastus sat on an overturned washtub in the corner. He was completely silent, completely motionless. Perhaps the blast had temporarily deafened him. Or perhaps his brain was now blocking out all sensory input, censoring the harsh, unjust world which was more than Erastus could now bear.

It was several minutes before anyone opened the door to his cell to check on him.

CHAPTER FOURTEEN

Theodore had never been sadder. Erastus spent most of his days now next to the new barn that Timothy had had constructed a few months earlier. Erastus carved wooden figures for several hours each morning. Afterward, he would line them up on a fence and then knock them over one by one. He did this over and over again, retrieving the wooden figures, balancing them on the fence, only to topple them once more into the dirt. He had been doing this since Timothy had brought him back from the town jail. Mrs. Dwight had administered strong tonics to Erastus to cleanse him of his melancholy, but her medicines had no effect on her troubled son.

Timothy had written a strong letter of protest to the Governor's office regarding the incident with Erastus. Northampton's constable had been severely reprimanded, and Alexander Barlow had fled, his printer's shop now abandoned. The townspeople had shown great sympathy and understanding toward the Dwight family in the wake of Erastus' detention. Theodore was quite proud of the swift and sure manner with which Timothy had dealt with the situation.

Theodore knew that Mary Dwight would not have been able to manage the situation. Her mood swings were more frequent, and Theodore found himself greatly concerned these days for his mother's welfare. Like Erastus—indeed like himself—she had been under great pressure during the past few years. And yet, despite the many tribulations of her family, she managed to run the household, albeit with a rather stern countenance on most days. He could not help but admire her tenacity. Cecil still would not leave the confines of the farm, but Mrs. Dwight taught young Cecil with a patience that she did not always exhibit with her other children. Cecil refused to attend Timothy's school because of his ever-present fears, and Mary assumed the sole responsibility for his education.

Theodore admired his mother. She could be overbearing at times, but she was an admirable woman, and he loved her.

Theodore finished his morning chore, pounding corn into meal on the hominy block, and decided to skip his noonday meal. He wanted to be by himself. He walked a short way into the forest and sat on a sycamore trunk that had been struck by lightning a few weeks earlier. A black scar zigzagged the entire length of the trunk where the bolt had split open the tree. Theodore passed his hand along the surface of the trunk.

Some things were permanent. A family could be terrorized, but its values could endure. A sycamore could be felled, but its weight and form and texture somehow survived. Erastus could be shocked from his senses, but a good heart would forever beat within his breast.

Theodore breathed in the stillness. He was alone—no Abigail, no Quinno—and in this deep solitude a thought touched Theodore's mind, a thought which would guide him for the rest of his days: he was a survivor, an individual of considerable strength.

Like his mother—and like the land itself—he would endure.

Chapter Fifteen

Endurance. Strength.

Theodore Dwight possessed both of these traits as he spent his days on the farm, surviving the harsh New England winters which brought knee deep snow and freezing temperatures to the land for weeks at a time. Erastus' condition had not improved, and Cecil, though he seemed happy and well-adjusted in most respects, still would not venture beyond the farm. The family's finances were improved, but Timothy was away from the farm almost every day except Sunday. Much of the workload fell on Theodore's shoulders.

The winter of 1782 had given way begrudgingly to the spring, wildflowers dotting dozens of fields by late April. Theodore walked back from town on April 29, carrying a sack of flour on his shoulder. The family's wagon had two cracked wheels, and it would be another week before Timothy could afford to pay Northampton's wheelwright for the repairs.

But Theodore's shoulders were strong, and he shouldered his burden on this breezy evening the way he carried all other burdens in life: with determination.

He brought the sack into the kitchen and dropped it carefully into the corner.

"You're late for supper," said his mother, not looking at him. She was clearly distracted by something, although Theodore did not think his late arrival was the cause.

Some things never changed.

* * *

"We have some correspondence that might be of interest to you," commented Timothy as Theodore took his seat at the dinner table. "From our Uncle Pierpont."

Mary Dwight shuddered. "I don't like hearing that name in this home." She passed bowls of boiled potatoes and fried pork to her children, her gestures stern and tense.

"Nevertheless," continued Timothy, "the matters he brings up are important ones regarding Theodore's future."

Theodore glanced at his brother, not sure what he was referring to.

"It seems that Uncle Pierpont proposes that you study law with him at some point in the future. Would that interest you, Theodore?"

Theodore rested his pewter fork on his plate. Law? He hadn't thought much about the future since his duties around the farm had increased so drastically. He had started to assume that the rest of his days might be spent planting and harvesting corn.

"I . . . I don't really know."

"Well," said Timothy, "there's time to consider the matter. But you're seventeen, and should you desire a career, it's not too early to speculate on what opportunities are most realistic."

"Of course he wants a career," said Mary Dwight. "But Pierpont is undisciplined. He . . ."

Mary rose and left the table.

"Pierpont is rather busy these days," Timothy's wife giggled.

"I think we might take the matter up at another time," Timothy said, looking at the inquisitive faces of his younger brothers and sisters.

   *   *   *

Theodore sat on his bed, thinking of the conversation he'd had with Timothy in the study after dinner to further discuss his uncle's invitation. Pierpont Edwards was a brilliant lawyer, and he was more than willing to have Theodore move into his home during his apprenticeship.

But Uncle Pierpont apparently did not devote all of his time to the law. Mary Ogden, Pierpont's sister-in-law, had just given birth to her second child. She lived with her brother-in-law and her sister. She was seventeen, unmarried, and both of her children had been named Edwards.

The conclusion one could draw was obvious.

Theodore now understood why his mother had reacted so strongly to the proposal that he study with his uncle. That adultery should be tolerated under the roof of a descendent of Jonathan Edwards was almost unbelievable. True, Pierpont was a man of wealth and influence, but such behavior might not—and *was* not—always accepted in other households.

Theodore would not be attending Yale. The money was simply not there, nor was he interested in becoming a divinity student like Timothy.

The law? He supposed such a profession might suit him. What fascinated him—what seized his imagination most of all—was that Mary Ogden was only seventeen years old. His own age.

Theodore stared vacantly at the wall, alive with shadowy figures produced by the flickering candle.

"Is this such a surprise to you?" asked Clarissa from her ethereal existence in the corner.

Theodore smiled. Mary Ogden was only seventeen. What *other* things, he wondered, might take place in the household of Pierpont Edwards?

"You cannot stay locked up in this room for the rest of your life," advised Clarissa. "It is not the kind of life for the likes of you and me. I tried to stay in my room to avoid unpleasantries, but in the end, the temptations of the dashing Lovelace were too much to resist."

There was a brief silence in the room.

"Besides," said Clarissa, "you have lived on the edge of life for too long. Your family still sits in the vestibule of the church. It is time to enter the mainstream of life."

"But I shall have to leave Abigail," Theodore whispered.

Clarissa was silent.

Theodore was aware that Abigail now attended parties and was seen in the company of various young men, most of them older than she. She was nineteen now. Still, she met Theodore in the forest, though not as frequently, where she continued to make a bed a ferns so that they could enjoy the intimacy of each other's company.

He would talk about this prospective move with Abigail.

After all, he loved her.

Chapter Sixteen

Bathed in shadow beneath the canopy of the forest, Theodore gazed into Abigail's eyes. Yes, he was certainly in love with her, thought of her constantly, dreamed of her. In truth, he lived for these moments, when he could be close to Abigail.

The shape which he had noticed underneath her blue cinched dress years earlier had blossomed. Her breasts had grown rounder, her thighs strong yet slender.

But she had never let Theodore make love to her, and sometimes he felt these hours he spent with her to be maddening. She had let his hands explore each curve of her body, had been generous in satisfying some of Theodore's other yearnings . . . but she would not consent to any true consummation of their affections.

"Do you love me?" Theodore asked as she rested her head on his shoulders.

"Why must you ask such a foolish question?" Abigail replied. "We are here together, are we not? Do not such actions speak for themselves?"

Several minutes passed—tense minutes—during which Theodore thought of many ways to express what he wished to say. He wasn't shy—his many imagined conversations with

Clarissa had long ago helped evaporate his nervousness around the opposite sex—but he needed the right words.

"Abigail?"

"Yes?"

"I—"

"Mmmm." Abigail nestled closer to Theodore and purred her breath on his neck.

"I'm contemplating a move to New Haven in the foreseeable future to study law with my uncle. It might be a splendid opportunity to establish myself."

Abigail giggled very slightly. "You've begun to talk with such formality, Theodore," she said dreamily.

"What I wish to say is this: if you wish me to remain here in Northampton for the sake of our love, I will."

There. He had said it.

A moment passed in which Theodore held his breath as he awaited a response.

But no response was forthcoming.

He shifted his eyes to look at Abigail. She had drifted into a slumber.

*   *   *

Theodore trudged over the forest trail that his footsteps had created over the years. The light of afternoon was fading, and the forest was darker than usual. Gloomier. Blue jays proclaimed the arrival of evening with their loud, screeching notes.

Theodore felt himself to be a fool. Clarissa had been right. He was a young man at the edge of life. Abigail Thorne was keeping him as a secret, a forbidden pleasure hidden by the sensuous greenery of the woods. He was a pleasant distraction on the periphery of her social agenda. She was clearly saving herself—what Theodore realized was her "formal" chastity—for the man she intended to marry, a young man who was part of the circle she inhabited in the parlors of Northampton, where bright lights and laughter and formal bows were the norm.

Theodore was younger than Abigail, and not as well off financially as her own family—or her formal suitors. She had cleverly avoided the question of her love, and it was all too apparent now why she had been evasive.

He sat in the deepening shadow and cried.

*   *   *

Every window of the Dwight home issued a bright light, throwing gaiety into the first hours of evening. The lights seemed to mock Theodore, who did not wish to think of well-lighted rooms or conversation . . . or Abigail.

A carriage sat in front of his home. Timothy was entertaining guests, and Theodore considered staying at the edge of the farm. He would prefer to watch the constellations wheel overhead instead of being forced to make idle conversation. This was the worst possible timing for forced socialization.

But no—Timothy deserved better. He had led the family out of perilous times. Even more importantly, Theodore remembered that he was a survivor. He would deal with the unpleasantness of the moment and stumble, albeit awkwardly, through whatever polite banter was necessary.

He walked forward and entered his home.

*   *   *

"Theodore, I'd like you to meet the Cogswells," said Timothy, standing next to the family's spinning wheel in the corner. "I met Reverend Cogswell at Windham, where I had the pleasure of preaching at the Congregational church in his parish. He is in Northampton to address certain business affairs today, and we shall have the honor of his company at dinner tonight."

Theodore smiled and lowered his head in a cordial greeting. "It is a pleasure, Mr. Cogswell."

There was no pleasure whatsoever in the meeting, as far as Theodore was concerned. His thoughts were still with Abigail Thorne.

"And may I introduce you to my son, Mason," returned Reverend Cogswell. "Though he is three years your senior, perhaps you two might find that you share something in common."

Mason Fitch Cogswell stepped forward and offered his hand. "Pleased to make your acquaintance, Theodore. Perhaps we shall have time to speak after dinner."

Theodore forced another smile. For Timothy's sake, he would play the gentleman. As Abigail had pointed out, he was capable of adopting a certain formality in his speech when it was called for.

*   *   *

Mason Cogswell was an intelligent young man whose interests were diverse.

"Study the law with Pierpont Edwards?" Mason asked incredulously. "You can't afford to pass up an opportunity like that!"

"You know of him?" asked Theodore.

"Most of Massachusetts and Connecticut know of Pierpont Edwards," Mason answered. "And parts of New York and Delaware, too, or so I hear." He burst out laughing. "There are some things that are rather hard to keep secret. Your uncle enjoys a bit of a reputation." Mason elbowed Theodore good naturedly as they walked leisurely along the dark road after dinner. The air was scented with wildflowers sprouting on the side of the road.

"You don't think it would be scandalous for me to study there?"

Mason stopped in his tracks, as if suddenly weighing an important matter. "Scandalous? Yes, positively, which is all the more reason you should go."

"Are you suggesting . . . " Theodore didn't know how to finish his question.

Mason laughed heartily, reading his young companion's mind. "No, no, no," he said. "I'm not suggesting you ravish any young hearts you might encounter passing through the Edwards' household. Nothing of the sort. But life would be . . . interesting, shall we say."

The two walked on in silence. It was Mason Cogswell who rekindled the conversation, again sensing Theodore's thoughts.

"The times are changing, politically as well as socially,

though my father is not altogether pleased with these changes, mind you. Be that as it may, there is a certain tolerance emerging for broader ways of thinking. Will the colonies gain independence? I think it is inevitable, for good or ill. Time moves on, and so should we. I myself intend to pursue a medical career and will study in New York, where I anticipate that life will also be . . . interesting."

Reverend Cogswell had entered the dooryard and was calling for his son to rejoin him by the carriage.

"The visit has been all too brief," Mason said. "Do keep in touch, Theodore." He winked. "And should you one day make that move to New Haven, I'd wouldn't mind a letter or two telling me of how polite Connecticut society conducts itself."

Theodore laughed and extended his hand. "Letters you shall have, my dear Mr. Cogswell, in the eventuality that I remove myself to the lodgings of Mr. Pierpont Edwards," Theodore said with intentional formality.

"Splendid," Mason replied.

*   *   *

Theodore looked up at the ten thousand stars dusting the night sky. The issue of Abigail no longer seemed so utterly dreadful. There was a certain pain in his heart when his mind summoned a picture of the beautiful young woman, but the past few hours spent in the company of Mason Cogswell had somehow made the pain seem more bearable.

Perhaps there were a good many more options in life than he had realized.

He walked back into his brightly lit home.

"Horsy!" demanded Cecil.

"Yes!" said Theodore. "Horsy! A long ride through the woods!"

Cecil smiled as the two brothers climbed the stairs to Theodore's bedroom.

Chapter Seventeen

Nineteen year old Theodore Dwight sat at a wooden desk in the last row of Timothy's modest schoolhouse, trying to focus as best he could on his studies, but he scrawled the same Latin words over and over again in the margin of his chapbook:

amo

amas

amat

The drudgery of schoolwork was allayed only by the wandering of his mind. Even in his Latin studies, he forever came back to "I love, you love, he she or it loves." He was a young man well versed in the classics, thanks to both Timothy and his mother, but his mind perpetually seemed to drift to thoughts of desirable young women.

He looked at the book again, but only a few seconds elapsed before his mind again escaped the tedium of study.

Northampton seemed smaller than it had before, smaller in some indefinable sense. It was as if Northampton was . . . on the edge of life, just as the Dwight farm was on the edge of the forest.

The forest. He spent less time there now, nor could he remember the last time he had seen Quinnohoag. His thoughts were of cities and parlors and bright lights and times that were interesting, as Mason Cogswell might have phrased it.

Life had indeed changed. Mason had been entirely correct. Benjamin Franklin had signed a treaty in Paris in February—four months previous—and ratification would surely follow. (Mason had predicted this in his latest letter to Theodore.)

The younger students in the room were growing restless since the instructor Timothy had hired had stepped outside to speak with someone. A boy in a butternut-colored shirt was busy chattering about a party at which he planned to kiss all the girls. Theodore was restless as well. He wanted to be by himself.

He slipped away without a sound.

*   *   *

There was absolutely no need for firewood currently. Summer was at hand, but Theodore needed to release energy, just as he had done years earlier when he howled like a wolf. He grabbed an ax and began to split wood feverishly for the next hour. He was a strong man—imposing, tall and muscular. He brought the ax's blade down with force on the wood—halving it and then quartering it—splinters and chips spraying through the air.

When there was no more wood to split, he wedged the ax in the last piece of timber and wiped the sweat from his brow with his shirt sleeve. He was hot.

And he was still restless.

He removed his shirt and climbed upon the uneven split

rail fence next to the woodpile. He balanced precariously, his arms extended fully. Instantly, he felt better. A slight wind tousled his hair and cooled his skin. His mind seemed sharp, and life's options seemed suddenly quite clear. On his left, toward his house, his mind's eye could see everything that had transpired in his life up to the present. He could hear his grandfather, Jonathan Edwards, as he promised hell to every soul which dared stray from the narrow road of salvation. He could see his mother sitting in the church vestibule with his brothers and sisters. And he beheld men talking—British loyalists—men opposed to independence for the colonies. Lastly, he saw Northampton, the place where he had spent so many years.

He looked to his right, his body swaying slightly but maintaining its balance, and saw a different world. Life without the British. Life without church services on the Sabbath. No preaching, no admonitions to piety. He saw his friend Mason, saw his Uncle Pierpont, and saw the city of New Haven. And off in the distance, he thought he saw Clarissa dancing in a meadow, carefree, her hair falling loosely about her shoulders.

Theodore closed his eyes and smiled. He was leaning more and more to the right side of the fence, to his visions of the future. Yes, he would have these things. It was time for him to take his place in the world.

And then he fell hard, landing squarely on his arm. A loud involuntary cry escaped his lips.

Cecil came running from the house immediately, his eyes wide. "Are you okay?" he asked, staring down at his brother.

Theodore winced. "My arm. I think I broke it. Get Timothy or mother or your sisters."

"They aren't here," replied a nervous Cecil, shaking his head. "Nobody's here. They're all in town." Cecil trembled at the sight of his brother.

"Erastus. Get Erastus."

"He's having his . . . troubles again. He's been in his room all day. He won't talk. Not to anyone."

Theodore looked at his younger brother. "I need a surgeon, Cecil. And quickly."

Cecil looked at his brother for an agonizing moment.

And then he ran up the road. He hadn't gone far when he ran directly into Timothy, who was walking toward the farm after several hours of labor. Cecil tugged on Timothy's shirt sleeve, crying out, almost dragging his older brother to where Theodore lay in agony.

Timothy knelt immediately by the injured young man. "Don't move," he told Theodore. "I'll get a doctor immediately."

Theodore smiled strangely at Timothy. "I've decided to go to New Haven and live with Uncle Pierpont," he said.

And then he blacked out.

Chapter Eighteen

The winter of 1784 was bitterly cold, but Theodore knew what he had to do before departing later in the day for New Haven.

He entered the forest wearing his heaviest coat. He walked only twenty yards before he heard a familiar call. It was Quinno, of course, for the woods were still and quiet on this cold, gray day. Birds did not sing on the bare branches which rose into the air like the fingers of skeletons.

"So Sapling—I hear that you are now ready to leave your home."

Quinno appeared from behind a tree, and he wore breeches, a cotton shirt and a woolen coat, appearing like any other man of the village.

"It has been a while, has it not, Sapling?"

"Why are you dressed like that?" Theodore's mouth hung open and his eyes narrowed in disbelief.

"One does what one has to do," replied Quinno. "My village grows smaller each year while Northampton grows larger. Hunting is not as easy as it used to be. I work for the blacksmith on some days. On others, I paint barns or clean privies. In exchange, I get food and clothing."

Theodore was horrified. A member of the Nipmuc

should be free to be . . . a Nipmuc. Yes, the world was changing, but Quinno's attire, his way of life—it seemed wrong. He thought of the nude maidens he had seen years before bathing in the waters of the Missonog. The freedom of the Nipmuc seemed to have dissolved. Quinno was no different than a black slave which some of the wealthier colonists kept on their farms or in their households.

"Goodbye, Sapling." Quinnohoag turned and walked away.

Theodore's heart sank. He had offended his friend by his reaction, which had been unintentional. No race of people, he thought, should be slaves to another.

Most of all, Theodore felt bad at having lost touch with Quinno for so long. What had happened to the years? He looked at the branches all around him, noting the absence of leaves.

The world had changed, just as the seasons.

Like Theodore himself, Quinno had grown older, and he had done what he had to do in order to survive.

Theodore left the forest, his spirit filled with the dread of winter . . . and change.

* * *

Theodore's many brothers and sisters stood in the dooryard under the gray, ominous skies. A few flakes of snow drifted through the air as the wind picked up.

"God go with you," said Timothy, hugging his brother.

"Will you be back?" asked Cecil.

"Of course," Theodore said, trying to sound as reassuring as he could.

Mary Dwight came from the house. "Goodbye, Theodore. Write often. And pray always." She handed him a package containing some bread and cheese for his journey and then went back into the house immediately, not turning back.

Theodore started down the road he had walked so many times while growing up. The snow was coming down heavily now, and he leaned forward into the wind to keep his momentum. He turned around only once.

Erastus stood at a second floor window. His face was expressionless, but he was waving goodbye to his brother.

Theodore returned the gesture and resumed his course. He couldn't bear to look at his family or his home one second longer.

*   *   *

Theodore waited for more than an hour at Docket's for the coach that would take him to New Haven. There was considerable concern because of the bad weather, but at last four horses galloped through the street, reined in by the driver directly in front of Docket & Son. There was a great deal of movement and confusion—baggage being loaded and unloaded, loud talk of conditions on the road, the sweaty leather harnesses removed from one team as four fresh horses were brought from the livery. The wind howled and the horses snorted, their labored exhalations filling the air with clouds of vapor.

Theodore moved forward, his right foot already resting on the first step, his hands gripping the black metal bars on either side of the door.

"Promise to come back," said a thin voice standing at the edge of the crowd of travelers.

Theodore glanced to his right and saw Cecil standing in front of the cobbler's. His little brother was alone.

"I promise," Theodore answered.

It was the first time Cecil had left the farm in almost eight years.

Theodore climbed into the coach and closed his eyes. It had been many years since he had uttered a prayer other than those that he mumbled on Sunday mornings when he was obliged to accompany his mother to church. But he prayed as the coach rumbled out of Northampton, shops and houses drifting by the window faster and faster as the horses gained speed.

It was a simple prayer: "Lord, look after my family."

The coach disappeared into the snow and darkness.

New Haven,
Connecticut,
1784

Chapter Nineteen

The home of Pierpont Edwards was a residence unlike any Theodore had ever seen. It was busy, but not in the same way that his own family residence had been busy, with his many siblings always about. The Edwards' home was dynamic, always in constant motion, with Pierpont meeting with business colleagues on matters of great import . . . or entertaining friends at dinner parties where it was not uncommon to have a dozen guests seated around the a table bright with candles and set with crystal, china, and silverware. His uncle was a man with a zest for living, and his speech was always animated, always filled with anecdotes and laughter.

The house itself was not opulent, but it was quite different from the relative austerity of the Dwight home in Northampton, which contained few pictures on the wall and few ornaments. His own home had been a typical New England residence, larger than most, but still marked by a certain spirit of utility and necessity. There were no carpets or drapes. The home of Pierpont Edwards was brightly lit with whale oil lamps, lace curtains and throw rugs and cushioned chairs. Portraits of ancestors decorated the walls, mirrors reflected the beauty of each room, and on almost every table were delicate figurines or gold candlestick holders or, to

Theodore's great delight, books. Pierpont's library proper was extensive, but everywhere in his home were leather-bound books, classics as well as more contemporary collections of stories or essays. A brass mantel clock sat over the fireplace in the drawing room, seeming to rule the residence by its constant marking of the passage of time with tick after steady tick.

Theodore's room was at the end of a long second story hallway. It was small, but private, and his bed was freshly made each day with clean linen by the black house slave, Louisa. Theodore was not accustomed to someone like Louisa attending to his every need, always offering him clean clothes or a meal if he arrived home late from his uncle's law office. He had difficulty accepting the fact that she was a slave.

Mary Ogden, Pierpont's sister-in-law and mother to Pierpont's children, Sarah and Horace, was extremely friendly to Theodore, taking him under her wing in order to facilitate his education in the more formal customs of polite society—customs of the table and dress and speech. She was a pretty young woman, though far from stunning. She had large blue eyes, high cheekbones, and curly blond hair which fell about her shoulders. Pierpont's eye was never far from Mary when she was in his presence.

A week after his arrival, Mary sat down with Theodore and took his hand in hers while sitting next to the fire as the stately clock marked the long hours of a particularly gloomy winter day.

"Promise me, dear Theodore, that you shall seek me out any time you have a need." She squeezed his hand. "I think we shall get along famously, you and I. My room is two doors down from yours. Never hesitate to appear at my threshold should you find yourself missing home."

Theodore was taken aback. Was Mary offering friendship . . . or something more? He didn't know. Her blue eyes held his gaze steadfastly. And her perfume—it was both exotic and intoxicating.

"Thank you," he stammered. "You're very kind."

The brass clock chimed six times, and by the last chime, Mary was still looking pleasantly into Theodore's face, smiling.

That very night, however, while lying in his feathered bed, Theodore heard giggles floating down the chilly hallway. He ventured timidly from his room and stood next to Mary's door. She wasn't alone. Every few moments, his uncle's distinctive laugh could be heard mixed with Mary's own giggles.

And an occasional exclamation or moan.

*   *   *

"Let us speak about the law," Pierpont said to Theodore a few days later while sitting in the large parlor on a particularly bright Sunday morning. Mrs. Edwards was attending church services. Her husband sometimes accompanied her, sometimes not, as was the case now.

Theodore sat opposite his uncle, straight and attentive in a wingback chair.

"The law," he said, "is a tool, Theodore. Always remember that."

Theodore nodded.

"It is an instrument to facilitate the resolution of conflicts. That is its ultimate goal."

"And it is very precise, I suppose," said Theodore, wanting to appear astute.

"Not as much as you might think, my boy. The law, I think, is to be practiced with flexibility and diplomacy. Like everything in life, it is open to interpretation. Each matter must be judged on its own merits."

"Everything in life?" Theodore asked, somewhat incredulously.

"Everything," replied Pierpont.

The front door opened and Mrs. Edwards walked through the downstairs hall with several other women.

"Even marriage," Pierpont said under his breath with a wry smile.

Sarah and Horace ran into the room, tugging on Theodore's arms. "Come play with us!" they pleaded. "A game of hide and seek! Please?"

"You seem to have won the hearts of my children," remarked Pierpont.

Theodore smiled. "It appears I have." He rose, thinking of how Pierpont had said "*my* children" without hesitation.

*   *   *

It was Theodore's turn to hide. He stood in a closet on the second floor. Behind him, he realized, was the master bedroom. There was a great deal of commotion coming from the other side of the wall.

Very *pleasant* commotion.

Pierpont and his wife were making love.

*   *   *

At dinner that night, Louisa filled his wine glass. Mary Dwight would never have served wine in her home, although Timothy had, on occasion, given Theodore a sip of claret when Mrs. Dwight remained in her room during dinner because of what she called "a feeling of indisposition."

Mary Ogden glanced across the table at Theodore. She could see the uncertainty written across his face. She picked up her glass, her eyes holding his, and put it to her lips. "Go on," she spoke silently, her lips forming words without sound.

Theodore lifted his glass. The red wine seemed mysterious, dark, forbidden—but also quite tempting as it reflected the dozens of candles burning in the chandelier. He looked again at Mary and took a sip.

The taste was agreeable. A tingling warmth cascaded down his body.

"A toast to Theodore!" urged Uncle Pierpont.

The Edwards family raised their glasses, and a feeling of warmth and cheer filled the dining room.

Theodore took another sip, and then another. He felt quite relaxed.

His life in Northampton seemed far away.

*   *   *

Theodore had not quite fallen asleep yet when there was a gentle tap on his door. He thought it might be Louisa, checking to see if he wanted anything from the kitchen before retiring, or perhaps an extra blanket.

It was Mary.

"I brought you something, dear cousin," for this had become her constant manner of addressing Theodore: cousin. She handed him a book. "It is *Orlando Furioso* by Ludovico Ariosto. It is very a very romantic Italian epic. I have noticed your fondness of books. I saw you reading *As You Like It* by Mr. Shakespeare. This poem also contains a character named Orlando."

"Thank you," said Theodore. Feeling a little lightheaded, he leaned forward to kiss Mary. At the last minute, he checked himself, realizing that he didn't know Mary very well at all. "Excuse me," he said apologetically.

"No excuses necessary, cousin," answered Mary, kissing Theodore lightly on the cheek.

* * *

In the mid 1780s New Haven was a bustle, reflecting the broad changes brought on by the American Revolution. The church-centered, Puritan roots of Connecticut were fraying. Some people were testing the limits in terms of general decorum, recreation and romance. Class division began to lessen somewhat. Drinking and gambling were on the rise. The sale of romance novels increased. Out of wedlock births rose. Church attendance dropped. Long held societal beliefs and modes of behavior regarding God, religion, sex and marriage were open for interpretation in some circles, including Theodore's uncle Pierpont. New Haven was very different from Northampton.

Orlando's Nemesis

Chapter Twenty

In Litchfield, Theodore was the last to exit from the elegant coach, following Pierpont, Mrs. Edwards, and Mary. He had never attended a ball before—certainly had never worn such formal attire—but after living for several months in the Edwards household, he felt quite comfortable as he stood in the warm night air, just moments away from his introduction to "society."

"You shall meet many fine young ladies tonight, my dear nephew," his uncle had whispered. "Try not to love them all at once."

Theodore laughed. Given Pierpont's lusty appetite, he was not entirely sure his uncle was joking.

*   *   *

Were there a dozen chandeliers in this great hall? A thousand candles? Ten thousand? Theodore was dizzy as he entered the large room, filled with a hundred people dressed in the utmost elegance and finery of the day. The men wore long dark coats, like the one Pierpont had purchased for Theodore the week before, and the women wore gowns—white, pink, blue—with elaborate embroidery and ribbons and borders.

"Come, cousin," said Mary, taking his hand. "It is time to

see how well you have learned the dance steps which I have taught you."

Theodore bowed and gave his hand to Mary.

There were no fiddle players here, per se, as there were at the socials in Northampton. There were violin players and cello players, dressed not too differently, Theodore thought, from soldiers—coats, brass buttons, and long stockings.

Mary had taught him how to perform reels and contra dances. These were formal steps which entailed men and women pairing together after forming long lines on opposite sides of the room. The steps were stylized, and only occasionally was Theodore reunited with Mary since the dances required a frequent change of partners. And yet, he always spun or circled his way back to Mary.

It was during the third dance that Theodore's life changed quite dramatically.

He once again started with Mary, but in the middle of the reel, he found himself with a young woman—their raised hands were touching only at the fingertips—whose eyes searched his face though she showed no trace of a smile like the other dancers. Indeed, her countenance was almost severe.

"You have been here a full hour, Mr. Dwight, and you have yet to introduce yourself," said the mysterious woman.

They changed partners.

Where was she?

More importantly, *who* was she?

He glanced over his shoulder, resulting in his missing the next step, but he was not embarrassed. The room was a blur of light and movement, but he was determined to find the face of the woman who had spoken to him.

There she was—on the far side of the room, and she was staring directly at Theodore. Her straight hair—light brown, almost blond—was parted in the middle, but sumptuous curls fell about her ears and cheeks, which possessed a glow of life that Theodore had never seen before in a woman. She had a vibrancy, a commanding presence.

And now—incredibly, wonderfully—the reel was once again moving her into close proximity to Theodore, who saw scarlet ribbons tied to the shoulders of her white gown.

That deep, rich color reminded him of the dark red in the crystal wine glass which he had raised when his uncle had toasted him.

She was closer still. Theodore felt as light-headed as when he had consumed the entire glass of wine after his uncle's toast.

She was just inches away now.

And then their fingertips were touching again as they circled each other. Theodore looked at the charming young woman, and she at him.

Abruptly, the music stopped.

"Do you not bow to your partner at the end of a dance, Mr. Dwight."

"I'm afraid you have me at a disadvantage," he said. "I am indeed Theodore Dwight, and you are . . . "

" . . . going outside for a breath of air, if you care to join me."

*   *   *

The April night was perfumed with the scent of azaleas.

Theodore and the young woman with the scarlet ribbons stood on the lawn, the light from the ballroom at their backs.

"And will you now introduce yourself?" Theodore asked.

"Perhaps," the woman replied.

"Perhaps?"

"You must first pay me the price of a kiss."

"Some would call that unseemly, to kiss someone without benefit of an introduction."

The young woman made no reply. She only moistened her lips with her tongue and blinked her eyes.

Theodore bent forward and kissed her lightly on the cheek. As he did so, he was keenly aware of how low the woman's dress was cut. And the scarlet ribbons—they contrasted so perfectly with the whiteness of her neck.

"And now?" he asked, his eyebrows raised in expectation. "You are . . . "

" . . . available, Mr. Dwight. I hope we shall speak further."

She turned and re-entered the ballroom, where another dance was just beginning.

Your neck is an ivory tower, Theodore thought, recalling the scripture he had memorized many years earlier. *You ravish my heart with a single one of your glances.*

Pierpont and his people, including Theodore, stayed overnight at a nearby inn. Theodore slept alone accept for his thoughts of the young women who captured his attention that evening.

*   *   *

"Did you enjoy yourself?" Mrs. Edwards asked Theodore on the way home the next morning. A was a day-long ride back to New Haven.

"He met the company of Miss Marianne Wolcott," said Mary, a broad smile on her face.

Uncle Pierpont looked furtively at Theodore. Theodore felt certain that his uncle's look was one of definite approval.

"She requests the presence of Theodore's company again next week at tea," added Mary.

"Yes," Theodore said, addressing Mrs. Edwards. "And I should love to attend."

He had no idea what Mary was talking about, but he was learning how to respond quickly in the very polite—and very fast—society of New Haven.

Mason had been correct. Times were definitely changing.

And they were, beyond a doubt, *interesting* times.

*   *   *

After their return to New Haven Theodore sat at the small desk in his room, far too excited to sleep. He dipped his pen in the inkwell and began a letter to Mason Cogswell.

April 21, 1785

Your theories have proved to be entirely accurate, dear friend The political changes in the colonies of late are indeed accompanied by a host of other changes, all of them entirely welcome.

I have recently met the most interesting creature who, I believe, has some direct interest in the friend who now writes this letter to you. She is lovely but most mysterious. She is Miss M. W., and she . . .

Theodore wrote for another hour. When he finally fell

asleep, the sun was already streaking the morning sky with brilliant flames of crimson . . . and scarlet.

Chapter Twenty-One

Theodore sat in the parlor of the Wolcott home, which was the equal of his uncle's in respect to its richness of decoration. The singular difference, in fact, was that Marianne now sat on the loveseat beside Theodore as he spoke of his family and Northampton, of his schooling and his apprenticeship with his uncle.

Marianne listened attentively, saying nothing, but as Theodore spoke, her hand covered his, which rested on his knee.

"Am I to learn nothing of Marianne?" he asked when he finished describing the many times he and Cecil had played together.

Marianne leaned over and whispered briefly in Theodore's ear.

For a moment, Theodore said nothing. Perhaps he hadn't heard the words correctly which she had spoken delicately with her lips no more than an inch from his ear.

And then a slight grin spread across his face. He had heard her quite clearly.

"Yes," he said. "I suppose that tells me a great deal about Marianne."

* * *

Theodore lay on his bed that night reading *Orlando Furioso*. It was a riveting tale that he could not stop reading, especially in light of the day's developments with Marianne.

Orlando was a knight, pure and true, in the service of Charlemagne. He was lured by the extraordinary beauty of a maiden named Angelica. But the fair Angelica married a wounded Moorish youth named Medoro. When Orlando happened upon them in the woods, he became thoroughly mad and ran naked through the forest, destroying everything he saw. Only later was he cured, when he finally returned to the camp of Charlemagne.

"And what do you think of Orlando?"

Theodore looked up, unaware that Mary had entered his room.

"I think he and I have much in common, for the very remembrance of Marianne's face drives me absolutely insane with longing to be with her."

Mary sat on the edge of Theodore's bed.

"So my cousin is smitten?"

"Yes, quite."

Theodore suddenly blushed. He had grown wiser to the ways of the heart in a very short time. He realized that his confession to Mary was perhaps a bit indelicate, given the familiar manner she had adopted with him.

"You don't need to blush in my presence, cousin."

"But do you not mind that I speak with such passion of another woman?"

"I confess to a certain amount of jealousy," Mary

admitted. "Should you and Marianne not have met, perhaps I myself might be pursuing you more diligently."

Mary leaned over and hugged Dwight closely. "But I am happy for my dear cousin," she said. "And I hope that he shall not be hesitant to tell me how things proceed with Marianne Wolcott in the coming days."

Theodore put his arms around Mary and held her tightly.

He had never known such kinship with a woman before, not even with Abigail Thorne. He had continued to write to Mason, but it was good to have someone in the same house who he could confide in.

"And when will you see her next?" questioned Mary.

"Tomorrow. She comes to New Haven tomorrow."

*   *   *

April 28, 1785

Let me tell you, my dear Mason, of a most extraordinary development. Miss Wolcott told me recently that if I would receive her here at the Edwards home, she had something of particular intimacy to give me. She whispered this sentiment into my ear, at which time I was most amazed— but pleased. You should not be surprised to learn that my imagination has not allowed me much sleep since these words were spoken.

Life at my uncle's is quite wonderful. When we meet, I must tell you of Mary Ogden, who is a remarkable woman for several reasons.

Yours,

Theodore

CHAPTER TWENTY-TWO

Theodore was quite agitated as he went about his morning's work in the office of Pierpont, cluttered with open books, which amounted to filing papers and copying letters. His apprenticeship thus far entailed quite a bit of such drudgery, though he did not resent such work in the least. His uncle was allowing him to learn gradually by exposing him to certain documents and teaching him various procedural matters. Often Theodore's education amounted to simply listening to Pierpont discuss things which would have been quite tedious coming straight from textbooks. He was agitated, however, in anticipation of his visitor from Litchfield later that day.

"I do believe that you have copied that complaint at least three times," commented his uncle.

"I have?" asked Theodore.

"Perhaps you should go home now," Pierpont suggested, smiling. "Lucky is the man who gets a visit from Marianne Wolcott."

Theodore left immediately.

* * *

Theodore stood in his room, facing the mirror, as he fastened the top button of his white silk shirt. Louisa had promised to prepare tea as soon as Marianne arrived.

The room to Theodore's room opened unexpectedly. Marianne Wolcott stood in the hall. "I was told I could find you here," she said.

"But—"

"Aren't you going to invite me in?"

"What if someone should discover us?"

"Mary assures me that we're quite alone, but do you really think your uncle would be upset should he find us in your room?"

"Perhaps not, but I don't know if others might be as forgiving."

Marianne walked to Theodore's bed and lay down. "Come," she said. "I have something to give you, just as I promised.

Theodore approached the bed and removed his boots. He sat down on the edge of the feather mattress and watched Marianne as she pulled a button off the front of her dress.

"For you," she said, holding the button for Theodore to take. The top of her dress opened slightly. Her modesty was not really compromised—much less was now revealed than on the night she wore her ball gown with the scarlet ribbons—but the gesture was seductive in the extreme.

Theodore took the button, and as he did so, Marianne drew him down and kissed his lips and his cheeks over and over. And then she rested his head against her bosom.

He lay next to Marianne for a long time, listening to the rhythm of her breathing. It was as regular—and as overwhelming—as the ocean's tide.

Chapter Twenty-three

The next two months were happy ones for Theodore Dwight. He studied diligently with Pierpont, his studies advancing in both complexity and interest.

But the chief source of Theodore's contentment came from the fact that Marianne was allowed free access to his room by the very lenient Pierpont. Pierpont, of course, was not alone in his more relaxed moral posture, for the practice of bundling, which Theodore had shared (though clandestinely) with Abigail Thorne, was widely accepted in some circles—lying next to the opposite sex with the presumption that nothing more serious would transpire than fond embraces or long kisses. Several times a week, Marianne was escorted to Theodore's room, where the couple enjoyed each other's company in a leisurely fashion.

But Theodore was also frustrated in many respects by these intimate sessions. He pleaded with Marianne to be allowed to make love to her, but she would not allow the consummation of their affection.

"But I love you," Theodore pleaded on one occasion. "Surely you know what a sweet torture it is to be so close to you and yet not be able to possess you totally."

Marianne looked tenderly into Theodore's eyes. "There

could be consequences to lovemaking, and we can't pretend otherwise. You know that my heart favors you, Theodore. Don't be cruel to me by begging constantly for something I can't give you at present."

She paused, and there was considerable calculation in the few seconds of silence, as if this moment had been rehearsed many times.

"You have spoken of your love, which is graciously received," she continued. "But you haven't spoken of a commitment. Perhaps the pleasure you seek comes at a price." Marianne lowered her eyes seductively, her lips slightly parted, the breath of her words falling on Dwight's own lips as the couple lay next to each other in the feather bed.

"But we haven't known each other long enough," Theodore protested. "A pledge of matrimony could be construed as a sign that you are *already* pregnant."

Marianne rose from the bed abruptly. "Think upon the matter, Theodore, and try to see it from my perspective. Another woman, less understanding than myself, might regard your behavior as somewhat . . . "

Marianne paused again for dramatic effect, looking at Theodore with a look of utmost seriousness.

" . . . selfish."

"Marianne, please wait! Let us speak further."

She descended the stairs quickly, exited the home, and looked up at Theodore's window briefly before entering her carriage.

Theodore threw himself across the bed and buried his face in the covers which still bore the scent of Marianne. "Happiness," he said to himself, "can be such a pleasant misery."

*   *   *

Theodore attended another ball at Litchfield the following week. Marianne greeted him warmly and laced her arm through his while talking with friends of matters decidedly unimportant—the weather and who had recently been seen with whom.

When it came time to dance, however, she accepted an invitation from a young gentleman who obviously was no stranger to the beautiful Marianne.

"I shall only be a moment," she promised Theodore, disengaging her arm.

There was a look of consternation upon Theodore's face.

"I must be polite," she gently chided him as she was led into a lively reel by the gentleman.

Theodore moved into a corner, remaining silent and alone. He studied Marianne as she wheeled through the room. She gave a warm smile to each new partner she met in the course of the dance.

When the reel was finished, Marianne did not return. Her attentions were given to one man after another, both in conversation and dance.

Theodore was angry, confused. On the one hand, her behavior was no different than it had been at the first ball he had attended. She was still an outgoing, enthusiastic person, but something was different. Was she punishing him for his lack of commitment? It seemed to Theodore that she was flaunting her good looks, shamelessly flirting with other men because he had not given her any kind of firm indication of his future intentions. She looked at him occasionally in the course of the evening, and he felt her looks to be affronts—*yes, watch me, Theodore, and see how much interest there is in me. Will you speak of marriage now?*

Theodore was quite miserable for the rest of the evening.

*   *   *

June 16, 1785
New Haven
My Dear Marianne,

You have treated me most cruelly by ignoring the plight of one who loves and admires you so. I am returning to you the button which you generously gave me two months ago. Perhaps it would suit you to give it to one of your more worthy admirers.

Sincerely,
Theodore Dwight

Theodore looked at the shadows dancing on the wall. She was there, of course—the beautiful Clarissa—and for the first time he understood that this sensuous, lovely sprite that had haunted his imagination for so long was none other than Marianne herself. Clarissa was Marianne, and Marianne was Clarissa.

"Why do you do this to me?" he demanded. "Why?"

The flame sputtered, dipped, and then rose more brilliantly than before, causing Clarissa to dance across the wall in the same fashion that she had wheeled across the dance floor at Litchfield.

"Because I must, Theodore. I simply must."

"Is your heart so hard? Can you take no pity on me at all?"

"You must give me a pledge of faithfulness, my dear Theodore," Clarissa whispered. "Only then . . . "

The flame was disrupted momentarily by a draft of air, causing the shadow to arc sinuously, creating the illusion of Clarissa's silhouette, her breasts displayed clearly for the imaginings of Theodore Dwight.

"Only then," she whispered again before disappearing.

Theodore sat on the wooden chair at his desk, his head in his hands. The situation seemed intolerable.

*   *   *

"Mary?"

"Yes cousin?"

Theodore approached Mary's bed. In the dim moonlight which entered the window and fell across the pale sheets, she could see the tears lying on Theodore's cheeks.

"Come, cousin," she said, sitting up and holding out her arms. The white linen nightgown slid from her shoulders.

Theodore fell into her embrace, pulling the covers over them both.

Mary's body was warm, and she gave herself generously—and completely—to her "cousin" from Northampton.

"I am always here for you," she told him when they

were finished. "Always."

CHAPTER TWENTY-FOUR

"I am beside myself, Mason," Theodore told his friend. They were sitting in the drawing room of Mason's brother, James, in New York City. The room was small, lending the conversation an air of intimacy. "She is the most maddening creature on this entire earth. And the most beautiful." Theodore paused to laugh. "What in God's name am I going to do?"

Mason Fitch Cogswell sat back in his chair and clasped his hands. "First, Theodore, I need to tell you that your experiences are not unique. You're not the only man who must negotiate the rather unpredictable waters of romance."

"You?" asked Theodore.

"Yes, me," answered his friend. "I do not exactly live the life of a monk."

Mason leaned forward to place another log on the fire to keep the chill away. It was a sunny but cold day in early October, 1785.

"You've got to put things into perspective," Mason continued, looking almost philosophical as he tried to console his friend. "We live in a new country, figuratively and literally. Read any history book and you'll see ample precedent for what is going on all around us. When politics change—especially when they allow people a greater collective voice in their own affairs—you can be sure that something else will inevitably appear."

He looked at Theodore.

"And that something else is this: affairs."

The two men laughed at Mason's little jest, which was calculated to make Theodore regard his problem with a little less gravity.

"But you take my point," said Mason, "that freedom is a bit like a piece of candy. One always desires more sweetness for the tongue. So it is in these times. Moral standards have been under attack for a while now, just as were the British. A political triumph now legitimizes other yearnings of the heart, so that people say and do things more freely which, only a few years ago, would have been condemned under our Puritan fathers."

"I fear that my newfound independence in New Haven is producing a bundle of troubles, confessed Theodore."

"Bundling," replied Mason, "is most definitely a potential source of troubles."

The young men laughed again, as all young men, attempting to understand matters of the heart, are wont to do.

The good humor of the friends was as much responsible as the hearth for dispelling the October chill.

*   *   *

Theodore and Mason approached New York harbor, passing through the teeming avenues of New York. More and more of the city's streets were now paved, and more two and three story buildings were now creating a broken skyline in several directions. Commerce was the city's heart, and the rigging of the schooners ahead spoke of a port that both welcomed and dispatched the freight of many nations.

"And so what shall I do, Mason? Any last words of advice before I find myself again immersed in Marianne's charms."

"Yes," said Mason, patting his younger friend firmly on the shoulder. "Be a gentleman, but don't give up. Love is a complex game. I would venture to say that Marianne's actions are perhaps an invitation for you to pursue her. And if all else should fail, it sounds as if your Mary Ogden is a delightful companion."

Theodore shook his head. "I wish Mary to remain only that: a companion, and I think that will suit her as well."

"In that case—do you, Theodore, take Marianne Wolcott—"

"Nor am I ready yet to commit to *any* woman," Theodore responded, rolling his eyes.

"Time will sort things out, my friend. Sooner or later, time itself decides what commitments will be made, whether as a result of our actions or the lack thereof. Go easy on yourself."

Theodore boarded the *Charles Drake*, the schooner which would cruise along Long Island Sound and take him back to Connecticut.

*   *   *

It was a dreary, dismal voyage for Theodore. His

fellow passengers were caught up in singing various songs, but Theodore continued to brood upon his relations with Marianne Wolcott. The waves rolled past the ship beneath a blue October sky, and Theodore thought that the monotony of the sea suited his disposition perfectly. He remained sullen and withdrawn as the travelers passed around a bottle of whiskey, which had the effect of making their singing both loud and off key.

"Join us, sir!" they encouraged Theodore. "Sing for all you're worth!"

"No, thank you," responded Theodore.

But they persisted for over an hour: "come now, and handle a verse or two, for we are as yet some distance from our destination."

Theodore shook his head and gathered his coat closer about his shoulders.

And still: "but we shall have a song yet from our silent passenger!"

Theodore sighed and stood, hoping to appease the insistent and somewhat tipsy passengers, who were singing a song called "Sophmonia." He feebly mouthed the words, not at all sure of the verses. Thankfully, the other passengers moved to a different song, after which they allowed Theodore to sit down again. Theodore felt foolish as the others smiled and danced across deck . . .

. . . as foolish as he had felt while Marianne carried on with others at the Litchfield ball in June. Once again, he felt himself to be a person at the very edge of existence. After all these years, he was still just an insignificant speck of life seated at the rear of the Congregational church in Northampton.

* * *

The following day, Theodore sat in a barber shop. He still felt melancholy, but a man was holding forth with story after story, full of mirth and animation. The people lining the walls of the shop were enthralled by his rhetoric as he puffed on a long-stemmed pipe.

Except for Theodore. He was reminded of the gaffers who sometimes sat along the walls of Docket & Sons, listening to the latest gossip. He wasn't interested in such light banter.

He was totally out of place, still very much on the edge of life.

* * *

That evening, he accompanied his uncle, who was a man quite respected in political circles, to a dinner attended by some of the members of the lower house of the Connecticut General Assembly. His spirits had rallied after returning from the barber shop. Just being in the company of Pierpont was sometimes enough to restore Theodore's enthusiasm, for his uncle was not a man given over to melancholy moods. Moreover, Theodore relished a good discussion, and even on occasion daydreamed of a political career. But the words of the speaker, Abraham Bishop, seemed lifeless. His ideas, to Theodore, possessed no originality, and he sank once more into despair.

* * *

It was late, and Theodore wished to thank Mason for his advice and good humor. He wrote several lines, relating the gloomy fifteen hour voyage home, the interminable conversation at the barber shop, the disappointing dinner.

He dipped his pen in the inkwell, but did not write further. The distant ticking of the clock somewhere below—the brass clock on the mantle, no doubt—accentuated the stillness of the night. A soft breeze stirred the lace curtains at the window. The weather had moderated in the past day, making October unusually warm.

It seemed as if he were the only one alive in the house that night, so quiet was everything around him. He was not at the edge of life after all. He was a man with a good family back in Northampton, and he had a promising legal career to look forward to.

He was life itself.

He finished his letter, apologizing to Mason for his somber ramblings.

He signed his letter Orlando. He was a little mad, perhaps, but such madness was normal under the circumstances. That's what Mason had been trying to tell him.

He would address Mason as "Edwin," should his letters fall into the wrong hands. He would refer to Marianne as Clarinda, but on this serene evening, he felt as if he could finally control his longings for the changeable Miss Wolcott.

Perhaps he would never mention her again.

CHAPTER TWENTY-FIVE

In late November, Theodore sat at a small inn in Hartford. Ever since he had heard the ticking of the clock the previous month while writing to Mason, he had thought more of his family back home. He missed them greatly, and he felt guilty that his preoccupations with Marianne had caused him to neglect the ones he loved so dearly. He intended to see them the following day.

For a few moments, as he lay in bed, he felt an eerie presence.

"Clarissa?" he called softly.

No, it was impossible. The candle by his night stand was not lit, and Marianne had not been in his thoughts for several hours. There were no sinewy, dancing shadows to entice or tempt his imagination on this quiet evening in Hartford.

But he did not fall asleep quickly. He remembered the many hours that Marianne had spent in his room. He thought of her scarlet ribbons, thought of the button she had taken from her dress in such a wanton fashion.

Marianne was once again close to his heart that night as he fell asleep.

*   *   *

Cecil was the first to greet Theodore, running toward him along the sunlit road leading to the farmhouse. His younger brother had grown taller in a short time. Even his voice was deeper. As for Timothy, he was overjoyed at the progress Theodore had made in his apprenticeship.

His mother called him into the kitchen after dinner. "Do you pray?" she asked her son. "Do your thoughts turn toward God in a house with the likes of your uncle?"

Theodore paused. His mother looked so much older and frailer. Even her voice sounded weaker. He wondered if caring for the family without his help was taking its toll on her.

"I can tell you truthfully, mother, that I am often in the company of angels when I am in my room."

His mother smiled feebly and went to her bedroom.

Theodore had momentarily forgotten how perceptive his mother was. It was likely that she had understood her son's meaning all too well.

*   *   *

"And how are you, my brother?" Theodore asked Erastus later in the evening. The two men sat in Erastus' spartan room, bare except for a bed and carved wooden figures.

"Tolerably well," Erastus answered. "There are nights when I hear voices." His eyes shifted back and forth nervously.

"I hear them as well," Theodore told his brother,

putting his arm around his shoulder. "It would be strange indeed if we, who are beset by troubles, did *not* hear voices once in a while."

Erastus smiled for the first time since Timothy had brought him home from the Northampton jail.

Chapter Twenty-Six

New Haven
December 1st, 1785
Last fortnight since I passed through Hartford, where was the lovely Clarinda. But I did not see her. Will you believe, Edwin, that your friend Orlando would go within twenty yards of the object of his most sincerest affection and not see her? However incredible, it is true, and in strict adherence to the resolutions he has heretofore made.

But what were my sensations upon hearing from her sister, who you know is buried in wedlock, of the very imminent danger the dear creature had been in by being in a chaise and almost delivered? Heaven be praised she escaped with a slight wound on her face.

I am yours sincerely,
Orlando

*   *   *

Theodore had been only twenty yards away from Marianne when he had passed through Hartford on the way to visit his family. He had learned that she had stayed at a home quite close to his inn. He wished he could go back in time and plead his love to her on that particular evening.

He had felt her presence there.

He was still deeply in love with Marianne Wolcott, and was that really any surprise? He was literally haunted by her presence.

CHAPTER TWENTY-SEVEN

Two days later, Theodore bounded up the stairs of the Wolcott home. Marianne's sister Laura had assured him that they could be alone for the next hour. He stood outside Marianne's door and knocked eagerly. If she would not admit him, he would enter anyway, even if it meant breaking the lock.

That wasn't going to be necessary.

"Come in, Theodore," said a silky voice.

Theodore opened the door immediately—and then froze in his tracks.

"I saw you coming up the front walk," said Marianne, her voice lilting and sweet.

She was wearing white stockings and undergarments and nothing else. She stood in the center of her bedroom, unashamed, as Theodore stared at the smooth white skin of her stomach, at the graceful slope of her shoulders, at the breasts he had dreamt of in many fitful dreams.

Theodore knelt in front of the presence which he adored and worshipped. He kissed her stomach and her hips, his hands wrapped around Marianne's waist, stroking the small of her back.

She ran her slender fingers through his hair like a comb,

massaging him and caressing him, and when he attempted to pull away to look up at her face, she drew his head back to her body and pressed it firmly against her middle.

"You are pure ecstasy and delight," proclaimed Theodore. "If there is a God in heaven, I pray only that this moment will last forever."

Marianne knelt by Theodore and kissed him gently as she continued stroking his hair.

"You cannot doubt my love any further," Theodore said. "Never again must you keep me at arm's length."

Marianne began to unfasten the buttons of Theodore's shirt. She was breathing fast, and each inhalation caused her breasts to rise and move forward against Theodore's chest.

A horse-drawn carriage stopped in front of the Wolcott residence. Footsteps raced up the stairway. There was an insistent knock on Marianne's door.

"Father has returned," whispered Laura urgently.

There was no answer within.

Laura knocked again.

"For heaven's sake," she cried in a low voice, "make some reply."

Within the bedroom, Marianne had quickly pushed away Theodore in order to reach for her dress.

"Promise me," he demanded, "that we shall finish what we started."

"Put your coat on, my impetuous lover," said Marianne, brushing his cheek with a feather-light kiss. "Then follow Laura. She'll take you down to the kitchen and into the parlor by a rear stairway."

Theodore straightened his shirt, donned his coat, and

stepped into the hall. He did not think he could calm his breathing should he encounter Marianne's father.

"Follow me," commanded Laura, taking Theodore's hand.

They disappeared through a doorway and descended to the first floor.

*   *   *

Laura and Theodore stood in the Wolcott kitchen.

"Come, Marianne," called Mr. Wolcott from the front part of the house, "or we shall be late in departing."

Theodore gazed at Laura with disbelief. "Marianne said I could wait in the parlor."

"My sister is quite distracted these days," Laura confessed. "Father and Marianne will be gone in a few minutes. They have an engagement."

Theodore's heart sank as Laura led him out of the residence. A few moments later, the same carriage that had brought Mr. Wolcott home was carrying Marianne and her father away. The light hoof beats of the horse faded, along with Theodore's hopes of possessing the fair Marianne.

Chapter Twenty-eight

Theodore returned to the Wolcotts two days later, filled with anticipation. The thoughts of pleasure which awaited him swam through his mind, making the journey in the chaise lent him by his uncle seem intolerably long. ("Love her mightily," advised Pierpont before Theodore's departure. "Make her sing for joy." Theodore had mentioned nothing of his intentions when informing his uncle of the day's journey, but Pierpont could clearly read the excitement in his nephew's face.)

"Please inform Marianne that I have arrived," he told Laura, who opened the front door.

Laura stared at Theodore for several seconds and then covered her mouth with her fingers in a gesture indicating disbelief. "Didn't my sister tell you that she would be away until tomorrow? Oh my dear Theodore! Come in and be seated."

Theodore sat in the drawing room, still not fully accepting Laura's news that Marianne wasn't at home. "I thought she would be home by now."

"She returned yesterday evening," Laura informed him, "but she left this morning with our mother to shop for dresses in New Haven. She will be home tomorrow evening or the next if they are able to find what they're looking for."

"Dresses? She's shopping for dresses?" Theodore couldn't believe what he was hearing. Surely Marianne had experienced the same passion as he, yearning for the moment when they could be together and steep themselves in the warmth of the other's embrace. Why hadn't she sent her mother off and awaited some word from himself, if not his actual arrival? He had thought of nothing for the past forty-eight hours except the softness of her flesh and the subtle fragrances of her body. She had held him so close to the very heart of his desire. No, it was inconceivable that she would not be at home, expecting the man that she had called "my impetuous lover."

He lowered his head to avoid the gaze of Laura. He felt thoroughly embarrassed and rejected.

"Walk with me awhile," Laura said, raising Theodore's chin with her hand. "It's a lovely day outside—far too lovely to sit in here and brood upon our misfortunes. My husband is away on business, and I should welcome some company."

Laura led Theodore into the spacious side yard, where there was a manicured path which curved through a fastidiously kept garden, with shrubs and benches affording privacy.

Theodore walked slowly by Marianne's sister, her arm through his, but his entire body still felt numb.

*   *   *

"Exactly what are Marianne's feelings?" questioned Theodore. "Do I stand a chance of winning her heart?"

"Marianne has great affection for you," Laura replied. "but she feels sometimes that you lack . . . a certain seriousness. She has told me on occasion that she wishes you would talk to her on matters of greater substance."

Theodore sighed. "Whatever does she mean by such a remark?"

"I'm not altogether certain, though I suspect she's still seeking some kind of commitment from you."

Theodore remained silent for a moment. "I'm simply not ready," he confessed at last. "I hope that doesn't cause you to think ill of me, but it's the truth. I'm not yet established in law, and to tell you the truth, Marianne herself seems to be far too . . . "

"'Frivolous' is the word you're searching for," said Laura. "And you have nothing to be ashamed of. Your honesty makes me wish all the more that it is you who my sister will one day settle on." Laura inhaled and looked up at the clear evening sky. "Assuming she ever settles at all."

Theodore laughed for the first time that day as they resumed their walk along the garden path.

"Since we're being honest," said Theodore, "may I ask you a personal question?"

"You may ask me anything, and if it's in my power to answer, I shall."

Theodore felt gratified to have a confidant so close to Marianne herself. Just being near Laura had done much to assuage his disappointment at not finding Marianne at home.

"You yourself have been married just a few months," he stated. "Do you have any regrets?"

Laura stopped walking and turned to face Theodore. "Yes," she replied, and then she resumed walking. "I'm feeling quite tired now, Theodore. I suppose we should be going back inside now."

"Of course," he said.

Theodore thought about his conversation with Laura on the way back to New Haven the following morning. She had not told him the precise nature of her regret, but he had obviously struck a nerve with his question. To Theodore, it was obvious that Laura either wished she had not married her husband, William Mosley, or that there were other things she wished she had done in her life prior to marriage.

The trip back to New Haven seemed especially long.

*   *   *

Theodore lit a candle by his bedside. It was late, but he couldn't sleep.

"Why do you torment me?" he asked Clarissa, who floated silently on the wall.

There was no response.

"I do not think you are ready for commitment any more than I," he said, "and yet you persist in demanding something from me that neither of us are prepared for. Don't you love me?"

Silence.

Theodore approached the wall and sank to his knees. "I want you, dear Clarissa, and I shall have no peace of mind until you open your heart to me without hesitation."

He kissed the dark shape flickering on the wall, his hand tracing the outline of the warm shadow. He leaned against the wall, but Clarissa didn't speak to him on this particular night.

CHAPTER TWENTY-NINE

Theodore was back in Litchfield three days later, though he did not go to the Wolcott residence. He was unsure of how to approach Marianne, of what to say or do. He wanted only, for the time being, to walk past the shops and homes of Litchfield, to be in the same town as the woman he idolized. Perhaps she would see him—see how forlorn he looked—and would emerge from a carriage and invite him back to her home, where she would comfort him and . . .

He felt ridiculous. He retraced his steps, moving past the same shops and homes, many adorned with Christmas wreaths. The town itself seemed happy, caught up in the holiday spirit. Theodore, however, was seized with melancholy. What was happiness other than tasting Marianne's red lips?

He rounded a corner and spotted Marianne twenty yards away. She had just emerged from a stationer's shop.

Theodore's heart seemed suspended in time, its next beat contingent on a dozen different possibilities. Was she with her mother? Would she look to her right and see him? Would he himself rush forward? Would they talk?

A young man exited the stationer's, the same man who Marianne had danced with at the Litchfield ball on the night

Theodore had left early.

"Oh Stephen," she giggled, "you are absolutely incorrigible. Whatever shall I do with you?"

Theodore turned and walked away hurriedly. He rounded the corner and slumped against a brick wall. He could think of no one in life that he detested more than Marianne Wolcott.

*   *   *

He went straight to his uncle's office upon returning to New Haven. He would immerse himself in his studies. He would force his thoughts into the dense paragraphs of some weighty book of codes governing the inheritance of real estate, force his thoughts into an avenue of strict logic and away from love and Marianne.

The words were meaningless. Not a single sentence made any sense at all.

He closed the book's cover abruptly and left the office, heading for the very outskirts of town. He paused at a meadow, beyond which was a grove of trees, still green despite the lateness of the year.

He wanted to be back in Northampton. He had been foolish to ever leave his family. He wanted to split wood until sweat drenched his body. He wanted to play with Cecil or listen to the voice of Timothy, always steady and reassuring. Even being in the vestibule of the Congregational church would have been preferable to standing on the edge of New Haven, alone.

Nothing had changed. He was still at the edge of life,

and he would remain so as long as Marianne scorned him.

Perhaps he would end up as Erastus, carving wooden images so that he could line them up on the fence, only to knock them over and retreat to his room.

*   *   *

He wrote to Mason, informing him of Marianne's latest affront. Were it not for the friendships of Mason Cogswell, Mary Ogden, and Laura Mosely, he thought he would surely go quite mad.

When he finished the letter, he lit the candle on his desk and stared at the wall until the flame had consumed the very last of the wax. The remains of two other candles sat next to the inkwell.

*   *   *

Abigail ran towards him, dressed in her blue cinched dress.

Yes, Theodore thought. *I should have pursued Abigail more vigorously.*

He was surrounded by the green holiness of the forest as he ran forward to greet her. Thank God he had been able to locate her—and thank God she had received his letter and replied.

They were in each other's arms, kissing each other with a passion that could have hardly been matched on any previous meeting in the forest.

Theodore ran his hand through Abigail's hair and drew

his head back to once again gaze into the clear liquid of her eyes. He found himself staring into the face of Marianne Wolcott.

"You've been quite naughty, Theodore," she admonished him. "My impetuous lover should know better."

Theodore sat up in bed, breathing quickly. His room was dark. No shadows, no Abigail Thorne.

And no Marianne.

Chapter Thirty

"It appears to be an invitation to a Christmas party," said Pierpont with great enthusiasm. "I presume you're going to attend. If not, let me know, for I hear there will be quite a few lovely ladies in attendance."

Theodore blushed. "I'm not sure if I should go, uncle."

Pierpont's countenance suddenly changed. "Have you been rejected in love?" he asked his apprentice. "I see upon your face the look of a puppy that has been removed from the litter and is pining for companionship."

"Not so much rejected as ignored one day and noticed the next."

"It is for such days that I live and breathe, my boy. Nothing like a challenge to keep one on his toes and feeling alive."

As usual, Theodore could not keep a straight face around his uncle.

*   *   *

On December 15, Theodore Dwight arrived at the Wolcott home at six in the evening, and was ushered into the parlor by Marianne, who greeted him warmly and kissed him quickly at the front door before taking him into the house.

The Wolcott home was decorated festively with red ribbons and dozens of extra candles. Guests spoke in lively tones of farming and the weather and, as was the case at most gatherings, politics. "Give us a Constitutional Convention," cried one of the older gentlemen, "so that we may have something more binding and forceful than the Articles of Confederation."

"Here, here!" cried several guests.

"A constitution would be most agreeable," remarked another, "and in the meantime, it would be fortunate indeed if someone would do two things: find a standard currency, and secondly, a woman young enough and pretty enough to be kissed right here and now!"

A young woman was pushed forward through the cluster of guests. "I will kiss you, sir," she proclaimed, "but only in the cause of liberty."

"If liberty is what it takes to get a kiss," said the man, "then let there be rebellions every day!"

"Here, here!"

The man was kissed promptly and eagerly by the young woman.

"And shall I not receive a kiss for the sake of liberty?" Theodore asked Marianne.

"I think there is an excellent chance, sir, that you will receive certain liberties before the evening is spent."

He wanted to ask Marianne about the man he had seen her with at the stationer's, but Theodore reasoned that there would be a more opportune time later that night—preferably *after* he had been kissed.

*   *   *

He sat across from Marianne at dinner in the long dining room as toast after toast was proposed and met by the increasingly merry partygoers. It was on the fourth toast that a certain Mr. Bainbridge advocated good health and an endless supply of wine. Theodore enthusiastically raised his glass and touched it to the goblet of the woman on his right, only to have his glass shatter, a shard of crystal lodging in his thumb. Marianne rose to her feet immediately and led Theodore to an adjoining room.

"Your high spirits are quite in evidence tonight," remarked Marianne, dabbing the spots of blood with a linen which soon became bright red.

Theodore smiled. Marianne's cheekbones were painted with pink blush which contrasted with the ivory hue of her neck and nose. She was a ravishing creature, he thought.

"You must let me be your nurse," she said, pulling at the splinter of glass.

"Ow!" he cried.

"Forgive me, Theodore. Repairing a wound can sometimes be quite painful."

And suddenly, the opening was there for the question, which still lingered in his mind. He had been wounded by the sight of Marianne with another man.

"That is true," he responded. "A wound can take time to mend, and—"

Marianne squeezed his thumb.

"Ouch! What are you doing?"

"Making sure that no glass is left in your thumb."

Marianne looked at Theodore. Her eyes were bright blue, pupils dilated, sparkling with the wine she herself had already consumed. "It appears that we may be running out of linen." She brought Theodore's thumb to her mouth and lapped the trickle of blood with her tongue.

Theodore said nothing, more than content to watch Marianne cleanse his wound in such an intimate manner. He had, in fact, already forgotten his question.

"I am a good nurse, am I not?" She kissed Theodore's hand in several places.

"That is the God's truth," he admitted in a whisper.

"There are so many things I could do for my poor Theodore," she said, now dabbing the cut with a few drops of brandy. "So many things I could do . . . under the right conditions."

The alcohol burned, but Theodore managed the sting with only a brief gasp.

Marianne pulled a white ribbon from her dress and wrapped it around her patient's thumb. "I seem to have spilled some brandy on my fingers," she said, licking her own hand slowly and sensuously.

"Is there somewhere we can be alone?" Theodore asked. He felt sure he had a fever, one which could only be extinguished by the most extraordinary attentions of his nurse.

Marianne pulled the end of the ribbon sharply to make it secure.

"Ow!" Theodore cried again.

"Is there something you wish to tell me?" asked Marianne. "Something in the way of a promise?"

"What I wish to tell you is—"

"I do hope your finger is okay," said Mrs. Wolcott, standing behind her daughter.

"Yes, it is perfectly fine," answered Theodore.

Marianne and Theodore returned to the dinner table.

*   *   *

"Good night, my impetuous lover," said Marianne, standing in the cold night air as Theodore stood by the carriage which would take him to a nearby inn because of the late hour. She took his thumb, still wrapped in her ribbon, and kissed it gently. "Sleep well."

"There can be no restful sleep unless you are beside me," he whispered in her ear.

She turned and walked gracefully back into her home.

She did not turn around.

CHAPTER THIRTY-ONE

He wanted to be near his Marianne, his Clarissa, his Clarinda—even if he were no closer than twenty yards. He was Orlando, utterly mad, and he had seen her only once in the past week, when her family had called on the Edwards home to deliver presents. She had been warm, had sat next to Theodore as the families had tea. She had gazed into his eyes, had held his hand. But she had left with no communication as to what he might expect.

"Be of stout heart," Laura whispered to him just before the Wolcotts departed for Litchfield. "My sister is quite fond of you—never doubt that."

That was sufficient to keep his hopes alive, for he knew that Laura could be trusted. In fact, he wished to be alone with her now, on this Christmas Eve, and find out what further details she knew of Marianne's affection.

Just twenty yards from Marianne. It didn't seem too much to ask.

*   *   *

Dinner seemed to last forever. He wanted to be back in his room, and when the family had finished exchanging presents, he went upstairs immediately in order to write Marianne a letter. If he did not express his love in some tangible way, he felt that he would explode.

Dearest Marianne,

Every thought on this Christmas Eve revolves around the memory of you and only you. You are the only star which I see this night, when tales are told of bright signs in the heavens.

That was no good. It was trite and sentimental.

Dearest Marianne,

Whatever you ask for, I shall give. If it is a pledge of faithfulness that you request, then take such upon receipt of this letter.

He stood and paced back and forth for several minutes. No, he couldn't give her a commitment. At least not on this particular evening. Perhaps he would feel differently in a day or two. He would think on the matter.

Dearest Marianne,

When our lips are close . . .

He wanted to make love to her, but he would not commit this very plain sentiment to paper and ink lest it be intercepted.

Mason had written him a few days earlier, encouraging him not to give up when he might be so close to attaining his heart's desire.

Dearest Marianne,

I give you, in this letter, my heart. If you, in your goodness, wish to give me anything in return, let it be a kind thought as you lay your head upon your pillow on this quiet night.

Yours always,
Theodore

*   *   *

Louisa knocked on Theodore's door. It was the day after Christmas, and Theodore had only been awake a short while.

"Yes?"

"This is for you, sir. It has only just arrived." She handed him a small square envelope.

"Thank you, Louisa."

Should he open it immediately? **Dare** *he open it? The contents of the envelope could answer his prayers or dash all hope completely.*

He pulled on the flap, breaking the sealing wax.

Inside was a piece of paper, folded in half. Lying in the fold was the button Marianne had torn from her dress and given to Theodore, the one he had returned to her.
The paper simply said "M."

His spirit was renewed.

Chapter Thirty-Two

Theodore called at the Wolcott residence three times during the following week, but Marianne refused to see him. She was, he was told, feeling indisposed. Theodore remembered the many times his mother withdrew to her room because of "feelings of indisposition" and doubted that there was any valid physical basis for Marianne's seclusion.

After his third attempt to see her, he returned home and wrote the following.

Dear Marianne,

I am most grateful for the button which you sent of late. Since you refuse to admit me to your presence, however, I enclose the ribbon you used to bind my wound at dinner, and I pray that if benevolence remains in your heart, you will affect a change of life.

Your humble servant,

Theodore Dwight

He loved Marianne, but it would be necessary to force the issue. She needed to be brought to her senses.

*   *   *

The shadow on the wall twisted and turned, holding

Theodore's attention long past midnight.

"Come now, Theodore," Clarissa said in an admonishing tone of voice. "You fell in love with me long ago, and yet you now disapprove of the way in which I demonstrate my affection. There was a time when you longed for my coquettishness. Do you not remember our first conversations in your room back in Northampton? You disappoint me, Theodore."

Theodore walked to his desk and blew out the candle. He would not be mocked by Clarissa.

The door to Theodore's room opened very quietly.

"Still awake, cousin?"

"Yes. Sleep is quite elusive on most nights. I fear I'm going completely mad."

Mary Ogden drew Theodore over to the bed.

"Sleep," she said, laying Theodore's head on her bosom. "Sleep."

He passed the night in Mary's arms, at times awakening to a gentle kiss on the forehead. "Sleep," Mary would repeat. "Sleep."

CHAPTER THIRTY-THREE

Marianne Wolcott sat in the kitchen of the Mosely home as Laura drank a cup of tea. "You're not well, Laura. Perhaps you should come home and let me look after you for awhile."

Laura looked up and wiped a tear from her cheek. "No, no, no! William would not stand for it. He says—" She turned away to finish her sentence. "He says that I must adopt a stronger constitution. He says my periodic spells of weakness are figments of my imagination."

"That is outrageous, dear sister. You need rest, not criticism."

"This is the lot I have chosen for myself," Laura said grimly, "and I shall not disgrace myself or my husband. The weak spells will pass. We have not been married a full year yet. I see all too clearly now that marriage is a question of adjustment."

"Adjustment? Whatever in the world does *that* mean?"

"One must adjust her expectations."

"And why," questioned Marianne, "must not William—or any man—not adjust *his* expectations?"

Laura stared vacantly at the kitchen hearth. "That dear sister, I cannot answer."

Orlando's Nemesis

*   *   *

Marianne returned home and sat in her room. It was a bitterly cold, raw evening, the air bluish-gray and damp. A pronounced sadness settled over her heart as she looked at Theodore's latest letter, in which he had returned the white ribbon from her dress. He was requesting that she change her life.

Requesting that she adjust her behavior.

In light of her conversation with Laura, an adjustment of her attitude was quite out of the question. Whatever her failings might be, she would have no man tell her what to do.

She looked at the other letter sitting on her bureau, the one from Stephen, the dear man who had been trying to court her ever since the Litchfield ball the previous fall. He did not kiss nearly as well as Theodore, but he was consistent and agreeable. He made no demands upon her, though he was clearly interested in the frequent pleasure of her company.

She would answer his letter, perhaps sending him some small token of affection in a communication requesting his presence at dinner the following week.

"Agreeable" suddenly seemed far more preferable than "impetuous."

CHAPTER THIRTY-FOUR

New Haven   February 20th, 1786

Clarinda is in very little danger of being neglected, my Edwin. Your Orlando has experienced an unusual serenity of mind for ten days past—a calmness to which his breast has been a stranger. Clarissa has at last proved merciful and would be wed. Last Sunday the bans of matrimony were legally proclaimed at Litchfield. The reason of my being silent with regard to her for so long a time is this: I have been in daily expectation of hearing that the Gordian knot is tied, and intended to have surprised you with the whole matter at one blast.

Yours,
Orlando

*   *   *

The news of Marianne's engagement to Stephen had devastated Theodore at first.

And then he had felt relief as he had never known it before. Let someone else deal with the changeable Miss Wolcott. Perhaps her future husband would be a calming influence upon her mercurial spirit, a spirit which had begun to wear on Theodore's own emotions to such a degree that he could not sleep for more than a few hours each night.

It was for the best.

*   *   *

Theodore lay next to Mary Ogden. "Do not deny me your favors this night. The winter is cold . . . and I am quite alone now."

"My poor cousin," said Mary. "My poor, poor cousin."

Mary lifted her covers and held Theodore closely.

CHAPTER THIRTY-FIVE

Not Stephen, but "Strephon." The news he had for Mason was both delirious and delightful, but he would not chance using the name of Marianne's suitor.

New Haven   March 11, 1786

On the day preceding her wedding day, her beloved began his march for the place which contained the sum total of his wishes, with his retinue having provided the necessary vehicles to transport his lovely wife to her destined place of residence. Accordingly, he arrived, when you may suppose he met his Clarinda with ecstasy, his heart beating high with the near prospect of possessing this pearl of great price, in his opinion as well as mine. But Edwin, listen to the sequel: instead of being married, a final and everlasting separation has taken place. As for poor Strephon, he spent his wedding day in exploring his way to Albany, for which fate he set out the morning after his fate was fixed. Before long, I hope to be able to furnish you particular intelligence in this matter.

Adieu,
Orlando

*   *   *

Theodore knew that Marianne still loved him. Why else would she leave poor Stephen at the very last minute. This was proof indeed that her passion, though restrained, was considerable indeed.

Could he be certain of this?

Clarissa assured him that very evening that his thinking was correct.

Chapter Thirty-Six

It was late March, and Marianne was restless. Laura was getting worse, and her husband seemed totally unconcerned about the poor health of his wife. There were days when she stayed in bed to preserve her strength, but he treated her malaise with contempt instead of kindness. The idea of marriage had suddenly gown repugnant to Marianne.

But she also felt quite alone. To avoid scandalous gossip since the severe "misunderstanding" with Stephen, her parents had advised her to remain at home. There would be no parties, no balls, no shopping for gowns.

Very well. She would not re-enter society just yet, but neither would she be confined to her home for an indefinite period of time. That would be intolerable.

She knew all too well where she could find comfort and companionship—as well as discretion and privacy.

CHAPTER THIRTY SEVEN

Theodore was both confused and delighted, but his delight was clearly in charge of his emotions upon learning that Marianne had ended her seclusion. She had sent him a letter stating that she hoped they might spend time together in the very near future.

He would redouble his efforts.

* * *

New Haven   April 12, 1786
Believe me, Edwin—Clarinda stands little chance if I should be all on fire.
Orlando

CHAPTER THIRTY-EIGHT

"And now you know the many pleasures of your impetuous lover," declared Theodore, staring into Marianne's eyes.

"His pleasures are considerable," Marianne said, pulling the sheet higher over her exposed skin.

The door opened abruptly.

"I was looking for Theodore," said Pierpont. "I can see, however, that the room is quite empty at the moment."

The door closed, Pierpont laughing heartily.

"God bless your uncle," said Marianne.

"May God bless him indeed," reiterated Theodore, kissing his lover tenderly on the neck. "Have I ever told you that your neck is like an ivory tower?" added Theodore.

"Several hundred times," Marianne giggled. "I should think a few hundred more will be sufficient."

She raised herself up on her elbow, her hair falling upon Theodore's chest. "Tell me this, my impetuous lover: why are there so many candles upon your writing stand? Exactly how do you spend your evening hours?"

Theodore smiled wickedly, but gave no reply.

"Perhaps you spend your nights with another lover?"

"There is no other, my dear Marianne. Be assured."

It was Marianne's turn to smile a wicked smile. "That is fortunate," she said, "or I should have to hurt you."

"What exactly would my punishment be?"

Marianne leaned over and bit Theodore on the lip.

Theodore flinched—and then laughed.

Marianne ran her fingernail firmly down Theodore's chest, scratching his skin so that a light red line was still visible a full minute after she lifted her hand.

"And does my impetuous lover protest such treatment?" she asked.

"He does not protest in the least."

* * *

Mary Ogden stood in the hallway, motionless, listening to the banter in Theodore's bedroom. She supposed she should be happy for her cousin. She *wanted* to be happy for him. But the truth was that her heart had been sorely disappointed when Marianne had resumed her clandestine visits to Theodore.

Perhaps Theodore did not realize how much she had come to love him.

CHAPTER THIRTY-NINE

New Haven   July 19, 1786,
I can never cease to see her in every moment's reflection and must discern her in every pleasing object. And yet, Edwin, I am at times spurred on to almost resolve upon measures that I know in my soul must forever deprive me of happiness. Resentment and ten thousand worse principles outreach me to this foolishness; but old Adam has great sway over my feelings—I have some small prospect of seeing this same Clarinda next week, and if not disappointed shall be then able to inform you of the ground I stand upon. But of this be assured—that three months shall not lapse before my Edwin shall be informed of his friend's situation with Clarinda, whether happy or miserable.
Orlando

*   *   *

Theodore walked along the streets of New Haven. Laura, who had been feeling somewhat better, had informed Theodore that Marianne had certain concerns at present—concerns that a woman in an indelicate position might have.

Marianne thought she might be pregnant.

Laura assured him that Marianne would do her best to see him the following week.

Theodore had not known such anxiety for months now, so happy had he been at Marianne's broken engagement and subsequent visits to Pierpont's home. He was not quite sure how he should feel. Would he be happy to hear that a marriage would need to take place quickly? Would he be relieved to have Marianne once and for all? Or would he breathe a sigh of relief upon hearing that her concerns of pregnancy had dissolved?

He looked around at the green foliage, the lush trees. He wished he were standing next to the waters of the Missonog, talking with Quinno, listening to the wisdom of his boyhood friend.

Or taking Cecil for a horsy ride.

Alas, the blood of Adam did indeed course through his veins, urging him to fulfill his every desire. And yet there was another temptation in his mind recently. Just as he had written to Mason, there were moments when he thought he should take strict measures to remove himself from the company of women altogether, at least for a time. His actions more and more seemed to be mere foolishness.

There was a rumble of thunder as a few summer clouds moved up from the horizon. For Theodore, there was judgment in that sound, just as there had been on the evening when the thunderstorm had moved over his farm after it had been destroyed by Patriots.

Yet another rumble echoed through the heavens.

It was the voice of Jonathan Edwards, was it not—preaching a sermon for his wayward grandson, who wandered aimlessly through life, governed by his baser instincts?

He returned home in a steady downpour. The lines of silver rain prevented him from noticing Mary, who stood at one of the upstairs windows.

She had been waiting to catch a glimpse of Theodore all afternoon.

Chapter Forty

Theodore did not have to wait three months. He saw Marianne the following week, as anticipated. She was not pregnant.

"You are quite free, dear Theodore," she told him, seeming surprisingly aloof. "I suppose you are relieved to find that you are under no obligation to take my hand."

"I am simply relieved that we are both free from a difficult situation," Theodore replied. "My love for you has not changed."

"I don't feel very well," Marianne stated abruptly. "The uncertainty of the past few weeks has taken its toll. Please excuse me."

Theodore was left alone in the Wolcott drawing room. A Connecticut cigar and brandy eased his wrenched heart. The floor clock ticked with his every heart beat.

* * *

"There are others," Marianne's sister Laura said plainly, as she and Theodore walked out into the garden and the bright mid summer sun. "She has begun to see other men, and I did not want you discover this fact by accident. I suspect that her own fears of commitment were accentuated when she thought she might be carrying a child. She now busies herself with a new round of parties and balls."

Theodore stared at the garden path in the side yard of the Wolcott home.

"It is no surprise to me, dear Laura. I anticipated as much."

He rose from the bench where they had been sitting.

"You shall remain in my heart as a dear friend," Theodore said, looking at Laura with both admiration and gratitude. "It is a considerable shame that Marianne does not possess your uncommon loyalty and honesty."

"What shall you do, Theodore?"

"What I should have done several months ago."

He turned and left.

Chapter Forty-One

September 11, 1786 was an unusually hot, humid day in New Haven. Marianne sat in the parlor of a home in New Haven with her brother Frederick and some of his acquaintances. As always, she planned on attending Yale's commencement that day. It was an occasion to be seen by so many handsome young men.

She was not altogether surprised when Theodore's presence was announced. It would be pleasant to see him again. She had wondered how he had been getting along since she had seen him last. In fact, she wished to invite him to a ball that would soon take place in Litchfield.

Theodore stood before her after a brief greeting to her brother and his companions.

"I have a letter for you in my pocket," he informed her, "though I shall not deliver it now, since you appear to be otherwise engaged. I shall send it to you directly."

And then he was gone.

This was not at all like her impetuous lover, Marianne thought. Not at all.

* * *

A messenger delivered the note later in the day. Marianne sat in a room by herself and opened the envelope.

Dear Marianne
I hope you will not be surprised when I request you, by the first convenient opportunity, to find me whatever letters of my writing you may have in possession—yours are enclosed.
Theodore

He was ending their relationship.

Marianne was furious. She rose from her seat and threw the letter to the floor. She paced nervously back and forth, her hands clenched in anger. How dare he do such a thing! How dare he reject her!

And then she sank back into her chair, her face in her hands. What would she do without her sweet Theodore? Of all the men she had known, he had been her most ardent admirer. No one had loved her more. She started to break-down.

She would hire a tutor—a preceptor—to instruct her in ways that she might control herself, ways in which she might gain an evenness of temper. She would learn the classic virtues: modesty, chastity, cleanliness. She would read prescribed books which depicted heroines who had overcome adversity. She would endeavor to gain strength of character. She would strive for obedience. Perhaps Theodore might reconsider his decision if he knew she was making a sincere effort to control her emotions and develop a stronger will.

In the meantime, of course, she would attend an occasional ball to rally her spirits.

CHAPTER FORTY-TWO

New Haven   September 20, 1786

Commencement is over, my dear Edwin, and I fancy you have a curiosity to hear something respecting it, especially as I expected to see Clarinda.

Friday morning I saw her, in company, as usual—she appeared to my interested eyes to be exceedingly confused, and I left her soon. In the afternoon, she was at a chapel, where there was a meeting. I sat in full front of her, and she scarcely raised her eyes once from the floor. Saturday she went home, but is to return again this fall. Thus, you see the matter is closed. At present I feel only easy and calm.

Yours forever,
Orlando

CHAPTER FORTY-THREE

Theodore's apprenticeship with Pierpont was finished. Until he passed the bar, he would teach at his brother Timothy's school in Greenfield.

His belongings had already been shipped ahead by coach. Theodore walked out the front door of the Edwards home for the last time in December, 1786.

Louisa brought Theodore some food for the journey.

"Thank you for your many kindnesses, Louisa," Theodore told the maid, hugging her. "Were it not for your steadiness and loyalty and hard work, this rather chaotic home could never be managed."

"Without steadiness," Louisa countered with a smile, "*nothing* can ever really be managed well."

*   *   *

"Farewell, cousin."

Theodore looked around, but saw no one.

"Do you not have a final word for me, dear cousin?" asked Mary, standing off to the side of the garden.

Theodore approached her, his arms outspread.

"My dear Mary," he said. "How can I ever thank you for

your friendship?"

A single tear escaped Mary's eye as she put Theodore's hand upon her breast. "Do not forget the beating of this heart," she said in a whisper.

"No," Theodore said, now visibly sad. "Forgetting such a heart as yours would be quite impossible." He kissed her on the forehead, and moved toward the waiting carriage very slowly.

In a moment Theodore was gone, but Mary stood motionless for several more minutes.

Chapter Forty-Four

"My dear Theodore!"

"My dear Mason!"

The two men looked at each other, expressionless . . . and then clapped each other on the shoulder and smiled broadly.

"It has been too long," proclaimed Mason.

"Yes, it has," agreed Theodore, "but there are not enough hours in the day to accomplish what one must. These are still . . . interesting times."

"And exactly what have you accomplished of late?" inquired Mason, tongue in cheek.

"I have imparted vast amounts of knowledge into the minds of dull-witted students at Timothy's school in Greenfield."

"And what of Timothy?" asked Mason. "Is he himself as dull as I remember?"

"Very much so—and as dependable as the day is long. God be praised for honest, hard-working people such as Timothy who offset the more frivolous behaviors of people like Theodore Dwight and Mason Fitch Cogswell."

The two men strolled leisurely across a green in Scotland, Connecticut. Mason had recently come from New

York via Long Island Sound so that he could talk with his comrade in person.

"Am I to take it that Theodore Dwight is still acting frivolously?" inquired Mason.

"Define frivolous," requested Theodore, laughing.

"The ladies!" exclaimed Mason. "You know exactly what I refer to! Do you still keep company with beautiful women?"

Theodore rubbed his chin. "Let me think. Well . . . "

Mason pushed Theodore's shoulder good-naturedly, sending Theodore backwards to the ground. "Out with it, Orlando, or I'll give you a thrashing!"

"Alright, alright," said Theodore, smiling and climbing to his feet. "So much for suspense. The answer is that I was frivolous on only one occasion. I was quite smitten with a comely young woman—the She of all "she's"—for a period of many weeks."

"Weeks?"

"Alas, dear Edwin, it was only weeks. Things progressed rather rapidly. There was innocent flirtation, followed by several walks in the evening, followed by not-so-innocent flirtation, followed by a great deal of tumbling and rolling, if you take my meaning, followed by a cooling of affections."

"I take your meaning quite clearly, Orlando. Why the sudden cooling of affections?"

"I believe," stated Theodore philosophically, "that the reason may be stated thusly: we both got what we were after."

"Tumbling and rolling?"

"Tumbling and rolling."

"Perhaps that is an improvement over years of emotional hide and seek?"

Theodore glanced at Mason. "I think just about anything might be an improvement over the moodiness of a coquette."

"Any news of our dear Clarinda?"

"She complains to friends of what she terms my 'abrupt requisition' of her letters. To this day, I still haven't received them."

"It is her way, no doubt, of wounding you one last time. An attempt, if you will, to retain the upper hand."

"She is now seriously involved with Harry Livingston," Theodore said, "though all reports say that she is gloomy and withdrawn."

"Lucky Harry," Mason remarked sarcastically. "Perhaps someone should warn the poor boy."

"Having been in Harry's position myself," answered Theodore, "I can testify that logic and reasoning are extremely hard to recognize while under the spell of Clarissa. Such a warning would be in vain."

"Do you yourself have any feeling left for Marianne?" asked Mason candidly.

Theodore stopped, looking earnestly at his friend. "I feel sorry for her. I'm afraid her flirtatious sensibilities will destroy her life. She ought to be married, but who will she have? No, my dear friend—I look on it like this: I recollect the pangs of puerile affection with a kind of pleasing satisfaction. It's over, and that suits me just fine."

He paused, then added "I'm certainly flattered when my name comes up in connection with Clarinda's, for she is a beautiful woman, and there are a dozen men who would surely kill to be in her company. Still, I would rather exist on my reputation as her former lover than exist on her erratic behavior."

"Well spoken," said Mason. "Which brings me to my final question: are there currently any others in line for the affections of Theodore Dwight?"

"Believe me, Mason, when I tell you I am currently content to think upon women once a week and no more."

"And in the future?"

"In the future I shall be delighted to continue thinking of women once a week, but I reserve the right to think upon them a good deal more. I'm not quite ready to burn all of my bridges just yet."

Mason smiled. "When your thoughts find a suitable romantic outlet, you are under strict orders to put such bounty into more letters."

"Bounty or no—you shall have letters enough, dear Mason. Our country is young and these are still interesting times."

The two men walked on, debating the serious matter of whether love made fools of men, or whether foolish men were simply more likely to fall in love. By the end of the day, they were able to reach no conclusion on the matter.

Haddam, Connecticut, 1788

CHAPTER FORTY-FIVE

Life in Haddam was very different from life in New Haven. By February of 1788, Theodore was living with Reverend Elizur May, his wife, and their nine children. Timothy had recommended the move to Theodore, and perhaps the suggestion had been prompted by Timothy's desire to have his brother live once again with a large, close-knit family—one that was decidedly religious. He lived in meager quarters—a cramped room with a bed and a table—which was quite unlike the generous lodging he had enjoyed with his uncle. There was no servant to tend to his every need, no Louisa bringing him fresh linen or late-night dinners. The May household ran on personal responsibility and hard work.

And there was no "cousin" down the hall to relieve his loneliness on long winter nights. Reverend May was a kind man, fifty-five years old, and there was in his faded blue eyes a look of understanding and acceptance which Theodore had never known in his life. This man was not someone who would abandon his family to seek greater fortune in Florida. Reverend May was, for all intents and purposes, the new father of Theodore Dwight.

May had four sons and five daughters. Three of the daughters, in their late teens, were distractions for Theodore inasmuch as they could bundle from dusk to dawn without their father's knowledge. There was much giggling, much creeping around late at night or early in the morning, before the sun cast its ever-present light on the actions of the May family. And yet these daughters were very dutiful, always performing their chores, always attending church services, always kind and beyond reproach when it came to their manners. Theodore thought that Reverend May must surely be aware of his daughters' surreptitious bundling . . . and yet the girls' father was filled with patience and understanding. Perhaps, Theodore reasoned, he ruled his household by example rather than stern lectures or harsh punishments. Still, the presence of bundling in the May household was unsettling to Theodore as he attempted to purify his mind of past indiscretions in order to steer a moral course.

The people of Haddam were simple people, many lacking in education. By the age of twenty-two they were usually married and well on their way to poverty, babies at the breast, and food bills gathering at an alarming rate. Theodore did not find friendship in this rural population. He felt himself above their mean, common lives. He was from better stock. His brother Timothy was well respected as a keen wit and consummate man of God, ruled by temperance. His maternal grandfather was Jonathan Edwards. While much of his extended adolescence had been squandered in rakishness, he had nevertheless been in the company of society, of his Uncle Pierpont, of the Wolcotts, of Mason Fitch. In Haddam, he carried on his duties under the law, respectful of his clients, but with a distance from those he served which was as much social as professional. He had relieved a young man of a shrewish wife. He had settled minor disputes over inheritance and the ownership of lands. God, he felt, had given him intelligence and breeding, and now he had been guided to the home of Elizur May. Surely God intended him to become a light in the darkness, a beacon of reason.

The Almighty had called him as his spokesman, to be a vehicle for the spread of moderation and discipline as the most important virtues of the Gospel.

* * *

He was strolling through Haddam, the sky having cleared after a late afternoon shower. A few men pulled a broken plow through the streets, taking it to the blacksmith for repairs. A pretty young maiden carried a bucket of milk from one house to another.

Laughter leaked from the doorway of a tavern which was perhaps doing too good a business for such an early hour of the day.

Theodore rounded a corner and found himself suddenly in the small town square, surrounded by young women who seemed to be most animated . . . and quite beautiful. Before he had time to retrace his steps and make a graceful retreat, a lovely creature with long blond hair had drawn him to the center of the square.

"Kind sir, please may we enlist you in a simple game called Button?" she asked. "It's a game which shall give you ample rewards for little work." She smiled, and for a split second, Theodore could have sworn that he was looking into the devilishly beautiful features of Abigail Thorne. But no—

Orlando's Nemesis

this was just a young woman from Haddam, one of the comelier maidens he had seen since his arrival.

Button. The very name of the game immediately summoned the image of Marianne to Theodore's mind, reminded him of the token of affection she had given him, the button from the top of her dress. He felt a longing travel down his spine. He shuddered and stepped forward hesitantly.

Theodore was given dozens of ordinary buttons, which he was instructed to lay in the dirt. As soon as he did so, however, several of the girls snatched the tokens from the ground and looked quite pleased, their faces painted with looks of self-satisfaction.

"To redeem your button, sir," they told him, "you must kiss us each as she commands you."

Theodore blushed. He had intended to get a little exercise in the late afternoon—not engage in foolish behavior with adolescent girls.

"You shall kiss me in the fashion of a wheel," said the blond who had pulled him into the game in the first place. "You shall take hold of my head as you kiss me . . ."

The other young women giggled uncontrollably.

". . . and turn it."

The blond stepped forward, and Theodore reluctantly put his hands on either side of her head. She pressed her lips against his, turning her head, her tongue twisting inside of Theodore's mouth.

"You shall have to do better than that, sir," she chided, "for it is I doing all the turning!"

There were more giggles as other young women stepped forward, offering Theodore their buttons, all requesting to be kissed like a wheel.

This was intolerable. He briefly smacked each girl on the lips with a perfunctory kiss, refusing to turn their heads like a wheel. But even innocent kisses were apparently all the girls required to pass a pleasant evening. By the end of an hour, Theodore's lips felt quite numb as he retreated to the home of Elizur May.

*   *   *

This frivolous mood was broken as soon as he entered the threshold and saw several men, their faces grave, assembled in the parlor. Reverend May himself was seated, his head downcast. It was Mrs. May who approached Theodore.

"It is our oldest daughter's little girl," explained Mrs. May. "She has a high fever. She rattles with each breath, and the doctor is not optimistic."

The Mays' oldest daughter was recently widowed. Theodore's new father and his daughter did not deserve this grief. He ascended the stairs and held the little girl's hand for the next three days. Her cheeks were blushed with fever, her breathing strained.

Theodore woke on Saturday morning, stiff from his all-night vigil, to find the girl's hand lifeless and cold. She was dead.

*   *   *

A week later, Theodore stood next to the child's grave. He had written the epitaph for the tombstone—two simple words which had moved the heart of Reverend May: "love endures."

He looked up at the October sky, the air chilly and unforgiving. The leaves of many of the trees had already turned. The branches of others were already bare.

Life seemed to be very transient to Theodore in that gray moment. He realized that over two decades in his own life had passed in the blink of an eye.

He left the cemetery, his collar raised against a rude New England wind which seemed to mock the very idea of kindness.

CHAPTER FORTY-SIX

Theodore was becoming a polished writer as the months passed. He still lit a candle each night as he committed his thoughts to paper, jotting down notes, writing brief essays, listing the constant flow of new ideas that daily ran through his brain.

He thought himself to be a poet of some accomplishment, and the fact that he could write of Marianne with dispassion, just as he had written of her in his later epistles to Mason, was further proof of not only his literary merits, but his ability to distance himself from his own past. He had survived the stinging love of the flirtatious Miss Wolcott, who had initially appeared to be so loving and sweet, innocent as a dove to his young and foolish mind. He dipped his pen and committed to paper lines which were proof of his strength and resolve, his ability to learn the more difficult lessons of the heart.

Ye swains who are subject to love
Whose bosoms with willingness yield,
When approach'd by the form of a Dove,
Burnace left a serpent conceal'd
For when, with an innocence too,
She soothes you beneath her soft wing,
Believe me you'll find it too here

Her down is the case of a sting.

He rested his pen and recalled how Marianne had come to his room at Pierpont's house, comforting and soothing him with a softness which had concealed her feminine wiles.

"Come, come," said a stern voice behind Theodore. "We'll have none of that."

"Who's there?" he called, turning around abruptly in his chair.

There was only a shadow on the wall, the very large shadow of a man wearing a greatcoat.

"You have come a long way," said the voice of Jonathan Edwards. "Now is not the time to be indulging in idle thoughts of your sinful past. You have more important work to do. Do you think that God does not know your heart? Your poem is admirable inasmuch as you are aware of the hidden dangers of romantic love, but you must put aside such frivolous verse in order to train your thoughts on more serious matters."

"Yes sir," said Theodore with awe and reverence.

The candle sputtered, and the apparition of his grandfather disappeared.

More serious matters? Yes, if he were to be God's spokesman, he needed to be willing to use his skills as a writer to expose injustice.

He took a new sheet of paper and once again dipped his pen. There was indeed a topic—slavery—he had been meaning to further deal with in verse, a topic which had never completely left his mind since the days he wandered through the forest near his home in Northampton, talking and playing with Quinnohoag. He still remembered the last time he had seen Quinno—dressed as a colonist and doing chores for a villager. And he remembered sweet, kind Louisa from the household of Uncle Pierpont.

In addition, slave ships now arrived monthly on the shores of Connecticut and the other colonies, carrying Africans squeezed together in abominable conditions. Many were unloaded like freight, having died from disease or starvation during the long, cruel voyage. They were human beings. That an emerging nation should seek to augment its labor through slavery and the degradation of human beings was morally abhorrent to Theodore. Jonathan Edwards himself had worked among the native Indians, shunning the idea that they were savages. They were made in the image and likeness of God, and their salvation was no less precious in the sight of the Almighty.

He wrote far into the night, revising his poem "African Mother," which had appeared anonymously in the New Haven Gazette in 1788. It had been the first anti-slavery poem written in the New World.

He was a member of the Society for those Unlawfully Held in Bondage, as well as the National Bible Society.

He found that he could not write fast enough each night as he honed his poems or wrote letters to those he was helping to disseminate the word of God by distributing Bibles as far south as Philadelphia. He was a man possessed with a fervor to set things right.

He did not notice that the shadow of another figure, that of a woman, still watched him on most nights from a corner of his room. He was far too busy.

Chapter Forty-Seven

Theodore visited Hartford as often as possible during the following year in order to visit Mason, who had finished his medical training. It was on one such visit that Mason introduced him to several of his friends, a meeting that would change the rest of Dwight's life. They were men of strong intellect, men like Lemuel Hopkins and Richard Alsop and Elihu Hubbard Smith. This circle of acquaintances was good company for Theodore, the perfect compliment to the pious, structured home of Reverend May. The men all believed that the government should serve the church. Society was built on stewardship, piety, moderation—virtues which could only be achieved through God's grace. Indeed, these virtues spoke directly to Theodore's heart, evoking his admiration for the land—the forest, the village of Northampton, his family farm. It was the simple life, one of honesty and thrift, which alone could curb the baser instincts of man, instincts of the flesh which Theodore knew from personal experience could be a man's undoing. The virtues of this simple life were also the virtues which should direct those governing the emerging nation.

The men were accustomed to convening their conversation in the drawing room of Richard Alsop, who next to Mason and his brother Timothy, Theodore regarded as the brightest mind of these exceptional wits. Alsop favored a strong federal government to rule the passions of the emerging nation. The group was delighted, for example, to have Washington as their first president since he was a man of resounding principle, a man capable of leading an entire army formed from men of such divergent backgrounds. As scripture said, a house built on sand could not endure, but the choice of Washington and Adams to lead the Republic through its infancy was tantamount to founding the government on solid rock.

It was on his second visit to the Alsop home that Theodore, sitting in the drawing room while Alsop held forth on the role that Calvinist tradition might take in keeping the various states politically cohesive, noticed a young woman whispering to one of the servants. He was mesmerized by the grace with which she moved her hands in explaining some point she was trying to make. She was unassuming but quite lovely. After a few moments, he did not even realize that Mason had switched the topic to the growing threat of slavery

"Wouldn't you agree, Theodore?"

"What?" said Dwight, released from his reverie. All of the men were looking straight at him.

"I believe your sister Mary has succeeded in getting the attention of Mr. Dwight," Mason said to Alsop. "She must be a rare woman indeed since Theodore is not a man given over to frivolous flirtation. Indeed, I have hardly ever known him to be distracted by the feminine form."

"My dear Mason," replied Theodore, "I do think you are a total and complete ass."

"That's the first sensible thing you've said all day," said

Mason, smiling.

Theodore laughed as he raised his head and stared at a large framed picture of the Connecticut countryside hanging between damask curtains. It was better to contemplate the painting than stare at Richard's sister any longer. Mason was far too fond of jests.

*   *   *

Theodore looked at the countryside outside of Haddam as his carriage rolled through late afternoon. He could not imagine living anywhere else. Farmers worked in their fields, shirt sleeves rolled up, their breeches caked with mud and dirt. Horses plodded through pastures as the sun rolled lazily through the sky. The Puritans had carved the first settlements from nothing with only determination and a belief in the hand of God. These farmers were stewards of the earth—hands of the Almighty reaching down from heaven to create his kingdom on earth.

This had been the preacher's message on so many Sunday mornings in his youth as he sat in the vestibule of the Congregational church. He had wasted his time, however, daydreaming about the slender Abigail Thorne, but that was in the past. In his heart, he had repented of the time he had wasted in pursuing the more worldly aspects of life.

*   *   *

He stepped from the coach to the hard-packed dirt streets of Haddam. The coach had come to a dust-covered halt directly in front of Theodore's law office.

"Hello, Theodore," said a familiar female voice. "I've been waiting for you for over an hour. I need to use your services."

Dwight remained silent as the coach rumbled away, leaving him face to face with Abigail Thorne.

    *   *   *

Theodore sat behind his desk as Abigail stared at him. She had blossomed in so many ways. Her eyes seemed sad, but they were deeper, darker. Her chest was fuller, her waist smaller, while her voice was as musical as the rushing of a stream. He thought fleetingly of the babble made by the Missonog, and suddenly he was standing beneath the birches and the sycamores, waiting for Abigail to arrive so that they might hold each other in the privacy of the forest.

"I need a divorce from a most cruel man, Theodore."

"I wasn't aware you lived in Haddam," he said, trying to focus his attention on the matter at hand.

She was so beautiful, so alluring.

"I live in New Haven."

"There are lawyers aplenty there," said Theodore, recovering his professional demeanor somewhat.

"It is *you* that I wish to handle this matter for me," said Abigail. "Besides, there have been enough rumors about me in New Haven."

"Such as?"

"Rumors of infidelity on my part." She leaned forward in her chair so that she could lay her hand on top of the

Theodore's, which rested on his desk. "But they're not true. They're all lies."

The touch of her warm fingers caused his heart to beat faster. His mouth was as dry as the dust out in the street.

"My husband has treated me most unkindly," said Abigail. "She pulled up the left sleeve of her dress, revealing a red scar upon her shoulder that could not have been very old. It crossed the top of her rounded skin, ending on her forearm.

Theodore's eyes narrowed. "Your husband did this to you?"

"Yes," said Abigail, now squeezing Theodore's hand, tears rolling liberally down her cheek. "Can you help me, my dear old love?"

Theodore cleared his throat. "I . . . shall look into the matter for you," he said, standing up so that he could remove his hand from the desk.

"I will post the particulars to you as soon as possible," she said. "My name is now Abigail Richardson."

Theodore smiled thinly as Abigail left. He sank into his chair, unable to think for the next hour.

CHAPTER FORTY-EIGHT

That night, he tried to compose a poem after tossing and turning in his bed, but he could only write a single word on the sheet of paper on his desk: "Orlando."

He thought it was Abigail's married name which plagued him so—Richardson, as in the author of his favorite boyhood reading, *Clarissa*.

"You can't just ignore me," pleaded the woman on the wall.

"Who are you?" demanded Theodore, feeling as if he might be going mad. "Are you Marianne? Abigail? Clarissa?"

"I'm all of them, sweet Theodore. You cannot just thrown me away like a used rag. I'm a part of your soul, whether you like it or not."

"No, you can't be," cried Theodore, slumping to the floor, kneeling in a posture of supplication.

"But don't you remember what we've shared?" the woman asked. "The times we lay in the forest? The times we lay in your room at Pierpont's? Don't you remember the button I gave you? Or how I removed the shard of glass from your hand? Don't you remember the waters of the Missonog breathing in the background while I let you explore my body?"

Theodore was now doubled over, unable to catch his breath. His sobs were choked in his throat, his eyes shut tightly as tears streamed down his face. There was a physical pain in his gut, a pain so sharp and so severe that he thought he would have to cry out for the Reverend May to bring a surgeon to his room.

"Begone!" said a deep thunderous voice.

The shadow tempting Theodore had transformed. It had grown taller and wider. The voice belonged to Jonathan Edwards.

"You must take charge of these unclean spirits, Theodore," he proclaimed in an authoritative voice. "Banish them immediately whenever they show their devilish faces, for they will tempt you as long as you are willing to entertain them."

"What must I do?" pleaded Theodore, trying to bring fresh air into his lungs. His arms trembled.

"Repent," said the specter of Edwards. "Repent."

"I understand," said Theodore, who removed his shirt and held out his arms in a cross.

He knelt on the floor until dawn, not daring to move. When the sun finally rose, he slumped over, his arms numb and his knees sore.

*   *   *

It was early afternoon when Theodore sat in the study of Reverend May.

"I must talk with you, father," he said.

Reverend May looked at his charge with steady eyes, aware that this was not the first time the young man had addressed him as "father."

Theodore was sweating, and he took out a handkerchief from his pocket to wipe away the perspiration from his forehead. "There are certain thoughts I cannot control. Certain . . . urges I wish to rid myself of, only . . . "

"Only you find this task difficult, correct?" asked Reverend May.

"Yes," Theodore said with shame, his head lowered. He could not bear to meet the eyes of the kindest man he had ever known.

"Have you read St. Paul, Theodore?"

"Yes . . . of course," he answered tentatively.

"In Corinthians, Paul says that it is better to marry than to burn with desire. God does not wish you to live in torment. Do you think I don't notice my three bundling daughters or hear them groping around in the night?" May smiled and sighed. "There is hope for them yet . . . and for you as well, my son."

This was the first time May had ever addressed Theodore as "son."

"You don't hate me because of what I've just said?" he asked.

"Hate, my dear Theodore, never accomplishes anything."

Theodore rose. He would go to his office; if he found a post from Abigail, he would decline to represent her in her misfortunes.

He wished his real father hadn't left him when he was a

boy. So much grief might have been avoided.

Theodore felt reborn.

CHAPTER FORTY-NINE

Theodore stopped at his office before catching the coach to Hartford. A letter had been left on his desk by his clerk. It was from Mrs. Abigail Richardson of New Haven. He lifted the letter into the air with his right hand, keeping it at arm's length, surveying it as if it might contain some chemist's poison. And perhaps that is *exactly* what it contained—a recipe for sin and damnation, a letter from Circe herself. It was no doubt a bewitching letter which could indeed turn a man into a base animal, a pig, a slave to passion.

He brought the letter close to his nose. It had a pleasing fragrance, some perfume to enchant him, to lure him into forgetfulness.

But he wouldn't forget his duties. Not this time.

He dropped the letter, unopened, into a larger parcel and addressed it to Abigail Richardson of New Haven. He wasn't the least bit interested in her plight. He strongly suspected that she had played no small part in whatever misfortune had befallen her. People reaped what they sowed.

He left his office and walked to the livery, where he would catch the next coach to Hartford.

*   *   *

Mary Alsop was a charming creature, or so thought Theodore Dwight. She was tall and thin, her blue eyes always lending her gaze a certain intensity. Her manners were quiet, but she was a purposeful woman. Whether she conversed with a friend or strolled in a garden, her movements were deliberate and her demeanor was permeated with self-confidence. Theodore had known many women in his life, certain dalliances having punctuated his more ardent pursuits of Marianne Wolcott.

That name—Marianne Wolcott—now caused Theodore to feel distant from his past, especially when he was in the company of Mary Alsop. She was pretty, but her beauty was far more austere than the extraverted Miss Wolcott's fairness, and it was this austerity which seemed to always hold Theodore under its scrutiny, as if Mary somehow knew of her suitor's past, knew of his former inclinations. When she smiled, her thin lips were always ready to retract their humorous indulgence in a matter of seconds. To Mary Alsop, life was essentially a serious proposition.

Theodore knew that Mary would become his wife one day. This was the kind of woman God had intended for him: someone with responsibility and discipline at the very heart of her spirit; someone who could keep careful watch over Theodore lest he stumble, as scripture said, and bruise his foot against a stone.

Someone named Mary, like his mother.

*   *   *

"So what do you think of our Mr. Washington?" questioned

Mary as she led Theodore down the streets of Hartford. It was late June, and the streets were lined with oaks, symbols of strength and permanence.

"I think our president is a person of unimpeachable character. He is a quiet man, but anyone who believes his tendency toward silence is indication of hesitation or weakness will soon find otherwise should he challenge Mr. Washington in debate."

"And do you know this for a fact?"

"As much as I know anything. My brother Timothy has been in the General's company on more than one occasion, and he steadfastly believes that no one else is suited to the task of leading the federal government."

"Richard speaks highly of your brother," stated Mary. "If your brother receives such endorsement, and in turn he himself gives equal endorsement to Mr. Washington, I shall regard it as fact that our country is in capable hands."

Mary's words were punctuated with logic. Her manner was formal.

Theodore was quite in love. He had never felt more liberated in his entire life.

Mary decided on a September wedding.

*   *   *

It was July 4, 1992, and Theodore walked into the meeting hall where the Society of Cincinnatus was meeting, the society being composed of revolutionary officers of the continental army. Dwight had been urged by his fellow Hartford Wits to address the gathering on this day celebrating hope and independence. He walked forward slowly but confidently, aware that the eyes of over a hundred men and women were focused on his tall, stately form. As a vessel of God, a mouthpiece of the Power above all powers, he was not hesitant about what he needed to say. He stood on a raised platform and spoke in a clear, commanding tone.

"France is a nation warmed with love and freedom," he began, alluding to the French Revolution. "The perdition in scripture of a season of universal freedom and tranquility, is rapidly fulfilling; a spirit of tolerance pervades all nations; and the religion of Emanuel is extending its influence over the regions of bigotry, persecution, and adultery."

Theodore's mood was one of exuberance as he continued his oration. In just a few words, he was uniting the will of God with political destiny. He also felt a great burden lifted from his soul at the mention of adultery. Though his speech was not a personal confession, he felt that he had atoned for his shameful indiscretions by publicly denouncing such immoral behavior.

Like America, Theodore Dwight had achieved independence and mitigated the energies released by it.

*   *   *

His true independence, however, would be celebrated for the rest of his life on September ninth of each year, for this was the day in 1792 that he was married to Mary Alsop. The ceremony was quiet and dignified, conducted by his brother Timothy at a small chapel in Middletown, Connecticut.

"We continue to live in interesting times, my dear

Theodore," remarked Mason Fitch after the ceremony.

"Yes, we do, for today we may safely say that Orlando is dead once and for all."

"And Clarissa? Is she dead as well?" Mason looked intently at his old friend, looking for some slight hesitation in his manner. He alone knew of the many trials which Orlando had suffered.

"That is an issue which only Chauncey Goodrich can answer," said Theodore. "Whether Mrs. Goodrich shall revert to her old ways as Miss Wolcott is a matter which he alone shall be forced to contend with."

"But if you were a betting man, Theodore, where would your money be placed?"

Theodore, feeling infinitely wise, did not need to reflect long upon his answer. "I should think," he said, "that there will be much high drama and histrionics behind the closed doors of the Goodrich home. If there is such a man, however, who is capable of taming his wife, I should think it would be Mr. Goodrich, who is an exceedingly good lawyer."

"One with ambitious political aspirations," remarked Mason. "He might even want the help of our group. Do you feel that you would be capable of aiding his efforts in light of his union with Marianne?"

"My dear Mason," replied Theodore, "Mary and I are moving to Hartford shortly, and we shall be neighbors of Mr. and Mrs. Goodrich. Should I encounter her, nothing would be capable of steering one away from the course I have chosen this very day."

"As I said," repeated Mason, "these are interesting times."

Mary Alsop Dwight looked with a certain amount of

suspicion at her new husband while they stood in the vestibule of the Middletown chapel. She did not like it when Theodore talked in low tones to anyone, particularly to Mason. She was aware that they had been friends for quite some time.

She suspected that they held secrets between them.

CHAPTER FIFTY

It was the fall of 1795, and the Dwight farm in Northampton had undergone surprisingly few changes. Corn still grew in four small fields, and the pig pen was just where it had always been. Theodore's sisters had married and moved away to nearby towns, but Cecil and Erastus continued to live with their mother, Mary Dwight. Mary was still a woman who prayed frequently and lived frugally. The house was immaculate, the floors free of dust, just as they had always been. The family Bible sat on a special table in the parlor. She hugged Theodore warmly as he entered the kitchen.

"I'm glad you haven't forgotten the path which leads to your home," she said. "A man's feet must travel—God knows—but sooner or later, they must always return home."

Was this an allusion to his father, whose feet had trekked far to the south, never to return? Was the death of Major Dwight still an open wound for Mary?

Theodore held his mother closely. She had grown frail over the years. While still an imposing figure, she did not seem to be as tall as she once was. Her hair was gray, and the lines etched across her forehead spoke of many grave concerns which she had no doubt pondered in her bed each night.

Orlando's Nemesis

*   *   *

"She still cowers from thunderstorms," claimed Cecil, who stood next to the barn, newly painted, in the crisp fall air. "I suspect she always will."

"Well, if it isn't my brother-in-law, the famous writer!" proclaimed a woman in her early twenties. Her hips were wide, and she filled every inch of the simple cotton dress she was wearing. She was carrying a basket filled with ears of corn from the corn crib.

"Hello, Ann," said Theodore warmly to Cecil's wife. "I am hardly famous, however."

"That's not what we hear around here," she countered, setting down her basket. "You political poems seem to be quite popular. Some are even set to music in taverns."

"And how would you know what kind of things transpire in taverns?" asked Theodore good naturedly.

Ann smacked Theodore on his rear end and picked up the basket of corn. "Even the Lord rested on the Sabbath," she chuckled, walking away.

Cecil looked at his brother with a certain sparkle in his eyes, the same sparkle which he had possessed years earlier when Theodore had given him horsy rides on his knee.

"You have a good life, don't you Cecil?"

"I wouldn't trade it for anything. Ann is a good woman."

"Does she attend church?" asked Theodore.

"Sometimes," answered Cecil. "She doesn't much care for sitting in the vestibule."

*   *   *

Erastus smiled when his brother entered his room.

"How are you?" asked Theodore.

Erastus stood and walked to the window. "There is talk of a revolution," he said in a barely audible voice. "Talk of independence from Britain."

He turned suddenly and advanced toward Theodore, grabbing him by the shoulders and shaking him.

"Always be loyal to the Crown, Theodore," he said. "Will you promise me that? A person cannot forget where he comes from."

There was desperation in Erastus' face.

"I promise," Theodore assured him.

"Will you be staying for dinner?" Erastus asked casually, as if it were the only thing that mattered to him.

"Yes. Of course."

*   *   *

The following day, Theodore stood next to the waters of the Missonog. They still sang lilting songs of the forest, which itself had not changed. He half-expected to hear the soft whistle of Quinno—was his old friend even alive?—but he knew that no Nipmuc village survived in the area. Cecil had informed him that members of the tribe had wandered away one by one, becoming more and more assimilated into American society.

More than ever, Theodore felt it his responsibility to protect his own family from dissolution. The land, his family, the tribe of the Nipmuc—these were sacred; they were meant to be permanent, with unwavering futures guided by steady customs and rhythms to ensure their preservation. As God's instrument, he would never allow his own family to be visited by trauma or insanity. And he would protect the land and this new republic, regardless of whatever personal sacrifices might become necessary.

He whistled softly and turned around, walking back to the family farm. There was no reply.

*   *   *

Theodore stood on the split rail fence in the exact location where he had fallen and broken his wrist years earlier. To his left was hearth and home—his mother, his wife, his country, his God. To the right was wilderness—the dim memory of Abigail Thorne and Marianne Wolcott and bundling and ardent letters composed at midnight.

He wasn't dizzy. He stepped from the rail carefully, lowering his body to the left.

He looked up at the trees. Some of the branches were already bare. It was fall, and Theodore Dwight was growing older.

*   *   *

The village of Northampton had changed. It was busier, for one thing. Commerce had increased. Far more people hurried back and forth, tending to a hundred different necessities in their places of business.

Theodore walked on. Docket & Sons was gone. In

place of the cobbler's shop was a tavern, though its doors were closed tightly against a fall morning wind.

He walked further, pausing in front of the print shop belonging to Alexander Barlow. The old bastard was still in business. For an instant, Theodore wanted to step forward and smash the front window of the man who had been the catalyst of his brother's madness. But he checked himself. As he stared at the printing presses through the window, he realized that God was speaking to him, calling him to a new career. He, Theodore Dwight, would indeed inflict damage, but he would do so as a righteous warrior. He would write pamphlets, exposing injustice and moral depravity.

He boarded a coach for Hartford within the hour. He was not a famous writer yet, as Ann had suggested, but he would become one soon enough.

Hartford, Connecticut, 1792-1815

By the mid 1790s the first two party system in the United States began to take shape. This party conflict was probably best exemplified by the tension between the Democratic-Republican, Thomas Jefferson on one hand, and his Federalist counterpart, Alexander Hamilton on the other. In Washington's Administration the young, brilliant, single-minded Alexander Hamilton was intent on forcing through his elaborate economic scheme. This scheme would promote manufactures and general economic growth as part of his plan to make the young country a strong nation that could compete globally.

Central to Hamilton's plan was an all encompassing, Bank of the United States. Among an array of financial functions, the "Bank" would fund revolutionary debt, establish national credit, regulate currency and deal with the influx of revenue from taxation. This revenue would be used to provide for a navy, standing army and internal improvements - roads, canals and the like. However, Jefferson saw Hamilton's broad plans as threatening to individual freedoms, impinging on state rights and a return to the British model of big, overly powerful central government. Indeed, the national growth that Hamilton envisioned was anti-agricultural and pro-business and manufacturing; in Hamilton's mind the farm was a

197

stagnant place where the best and brightest would languish. Hamilton's Bank would serve as the economic hub of an economy teaming with money to encourage young strivers to invent and create in the growing urban centers. Conversely, Jefferson saw the cities as centers of vice and corruption and the farm as the bastion of virtue, a view that proved ironic at best to his Federalist counterparts, Hamilton the most well known of these.

To many Federalists, old and young, Jefferson came to symbolize the problem of aristocratic Southern farming. Jefferson never worked his own farm, his slaves did. Jefferson lived beyond his means and was in perpetual debt. In fact, shortly after his death on July 4, 1826 Jefferson's slaves were auctioned off on the front lawn of Monticello to help pay his debts, which were never fully paid. Federalist John Adams died the same day exactly fifty years after the signing of the Declaration of Independence, which was composed by both men. In contrast, John Adams left land and over one hundred thousand dollars to his heirs. So, virtue as reflected through the handling of money, which meant continued dependence on slave labor, Jefferson fell short. He also fell short in terms of his racist views toward African Americans; he believed that African Americans were inherently inferior. And lastly, Jefferson had sex with some of his female slaves and fathered children with one in particular, Sally Hemmings. More than a few Federalists were aware of his life style as far back as the 1790s and thus saw Jefferson as hypocritical and a rabble rouser.

Theodore Dwight was one such Federalist. Reborn

and fortified with God's grace, Dwight would do battle with Jefferson and his followers in an effort to save his country and somehow get back at the revolutionaries who ransacked his family farm. Now he had the courage.

Chapter Fifty-One

In the spring of 1800, Theodore sat at his desk at the rear of the old stationer's shop which the Federalist Party had rented as its center in Hartford. He looked up at Ezekiel Charles Hood, who stood before him, waiting for his orders.

"Our goal," Theodore said, "is to talk to at least fifty voters each and every day. Spend time with them. Talk of the weather. Talk of their young daughters and their prospects for marriage. Talk about anything that will gain their attention and trust."

Hood nodded.

"Vice President Adams is our first candidate for President in the election of 1800. The second candidate of the party will be Thomas Pinckney."

Hood nodded his head again. He sat next to the hearth, the only source of warmth on the cold October morning. "He's from South Carolina. I'm not interested in promoting a southern planter for the presidency or vice presidency. This is complete madness, Theodore."

Theodore leaned forward in his chair and spoke, his voice steel. "Perhaps his candidacy doesn't suit you, but it suits Hamilton well enough. Pinckney will do anything Hamilton tells him to, and that's what matters—nothing else, do you understand? Adams is a good man, but he is a moderate in too many matters. He'll need a little . . . coaxing, shall we say. When you speak to voters, therefore, you tell them that Pinckney is a man above reproach, a man of God."

"How can this kind of idle religious conversation make any difference in an election?" asked Hood.

Theodore brought his fist down on the desk. "If God can't win an election, then no one can!" he shouted. "Now do as I tell you! Say whatever you have to say about Pinckney. Tell people that he'll personally kiss their daughters and employ their sons, if that's what it takes."

Hood left, putting on his heavy coat and wide-brimmed hat.

The fire in the hearth blazed. The shadow of an imposing man on the opposite wall seemed pleased at the thunderous tone of Dwight's tirade. The shadow thought he might have made a pretty fair preacher.

*   *   *

Theodore began writing the pamphlet that a printer's apprentice would set and distribute the following day. He knew exactly what he wanted to say, what he *needed* to say.

He published poems and circulars in newspapers that he edited, and which were political instruments of the Federalist party. He wrote the following with the same passion that he had used in his letters to Cogswell about Clarissa, except now his passion was dictated by righteousness.

ON THE MORAL CHARACTER OF THOMAS

JEFFERSON:

Since Mr. Jefferson will represent the Democratic-Republicans as candidate for President, the following should be regarded as wholly pertinent in the consideration of his qualifications.

It should not be forgotten that Mr. Jefferson resigned as Secretary of State when he could no longer tolerate the views of Mr. Washington. Mr. Jefferson persists in his views that French liberty in some way calls for a sympathetic emotional response simply because our own nation was spurred to revolution in the past. If he favors such bloodletting while turning a deaf ear to our relatives in England, he must be regarded with a great deal of suspicion and his loyalties must be seriously held in question. Indeed, his permissive and cavalier attitudes in matters of state are reflected in his very own life, such matters being well known to most citizens who have ears to hear the truth. A man who disregards the ties of marriage and consorts with mistresses kept within his own household is an abomination and is below the sacred trust which we lend when we give our assent to such a man as public servant. Such a man, by his own actions, proves himself to be an atheist and an adulterer.

Like most of his Federalist counterparts, Theodore saw the French Revolution as initially good. But after 1791, when it became more and more violent, most Federalists thought it became too radical. Liberty was all well and good, but anarchy and moral depravity was another. Most Federalists also distrusted Napoleon. By 1800 most Federalists took sides with the English, while many Southern planters, many of whom were in perpetual debt to British financial houses, were pro French. Moreover, it was generally believed that many of the French were morally corrupt and irreligious. Jefferson was pro French.

*   *   *

When he had finished his work for the day, Theodore walked home under a dreary sky in Hartford. His head was pounding, and it seemed as if he now lived with an endless headache. He arrived home, and as was so often his custom, he sat in a dark room to protect his eyes from the glare. Sound and light only made the pain worse.

Chapter Fifty-Two

And then the bad dreams started.

Theodore was sitting on the deck of a schooner, feeling forlorn about Marianne Wolcott despite his recent visit with Mason Cogswell Fitch in New York City. Passengers were asking him to sing—rude and persistent people who wouldn't let him be alone with his thoughts. The intense yellow light of the sun, together with the drunken tunes of his fellow travelers, was giving him a headache.

He got to his feet and staggered away from the crowd of insistent voices. Hanging from one of the masts was his father, twisting lifelessly in the brisk wind. His face was pale, drained of blood.

"This is what happens to the unfaithful," said his grandfather, walking up to Theodore as he looked in horror at the body of his father. "Do not abandon your country, Theodore, or leave her to her godless habits. Do not let her be ruled by adulterers and infidels."

"No," Theodore said, his mind dazed. "I will protect my home and my family."

The ship plowed through the waves, Theodore staring at the horizon and the endless rolling ocean.

*   *   *

He was waiting for Quinno, who was going to teach him how to howl like a wolf.

Abigail Thorne appeared instead, wearing a blue dress cinched at the waist. "I need your legal services, dearest Theodore," she said enticingly. "I've seen you staring at me in church, and I know you want to kiss me."

She held out her hand, and Theodore felt powerless against the wild beauty which he could not separate in his mind from the wildness of the forest.

"You know what you must do," whispered Quinno, hidden in the brush to his left.

"Do?"

"Yes, sapling" replied Quinno, handing Theodore a bow, an arrow already notched in the string.

Theodore took the bow and aimed the arrow straight at the heart of Abigail Thorne. Her immoral behavior had to be stopped. The temptation was too much to bear.

But how could he bring himself to let the arrow fly. He loved the beautiful Abigail, did he not?

"Shoot," said Quinno. "You're wasting time."

Theodore pulled back the bowstring and released the arrow. It whistled through the air, but he couldn't tell if it had found its mark. Night had mysteriously descended on the forest.

He was standing in blackness.

*   *   *

He lay next to Marianne, who had been escorted to his

room by Louisa. The black servant had look displeased. There was judgment in the face of the woman who tended to her chores so obediently each and every day in the home of Pierpont Edwards.

"Kiss me, Orlando," said Marianne. "Kiss me in the fashion of a wheel. Take my head in your sweet hands and turn it."

Theodore did as he was told. Marianne's body was soft and yielding, beneath his own. His tongue met hers—"

And then she opened her eyes wide, a maniacal grin on her face. Buttons were pouring from her mouth, causing Theodore to retreat and jump to his feet, staring at the grotesque creature on the bed. This was macabre—it was more than he could bear.

He left the room at once and ran down the hall into Mary Ogden's room.

"I've been waiting for you, cousin," Mary said. "You left me so many years ago. Surely you knew of the affection I had for you. Why did you leave me, Theodore? It was you I loved—not your uncle. You abandoned me, just as your father abandoned your mother. But you're back now, my love. Come closer, for the night is dreary and cold."

She pulled Theodore on top of her.

He wanted to say "no," but he could not move his muscles or utter a single word.

The door flew open, the knob shattering the plaster on the wall before bouncing back, restrained by the strong hand of Pierpont Edwards.

"Plow the field, young Theodore," he roared, laughing. "You are, after all, my apprentice, and if I can teach you nothing else, it is this: love with all your heart. Love endures!"

*   *   *

He was alone in the cemetery, sitting next to the gravestone. The epitaph for Reverend May's daughter said only "love endures."

Theodore looked up at the bare branches of the trees. More leaves had fallen than he had realized. Life was slipping through his fingers, but at least there was love—at least *something* endured.

*   *   *

The land was barren and cold. It was only October, but the hills were an ugly brown, the trees upon their slopes blasted or burned. A mob somewhere below was chanting in French. The people were demanding something, though Theodore didn't know at first what they wanted.

Independence. They wanted freedom.

Clarissa approached him from behind. "Love me, Theodore, or else I shall be forced to take drastic measures to gain what I want. I must be freed from this brothel or else I shall surely perish."

She produced a knife from the sleeve of her dress, and before Theodore could reach her, she cut her wrist.

Blood flowed liberally from her arm, becoming a river that filled the valleys between the brown, French hillsides.

"Freedom!" the mob screamed. "Freedom!"

Theodore yelled at the top of his lungs, sitting bolt

upright in their bed.

"Shhh," whispered Mary. "You're just having one of your nightmares again."

He lay back down, cradled by the arms of his wife. He was safe. He was in their bedroom in Hartford.

He fell into a dreamless sleep until morning, which is what always happened after the last nightmare had faded.

*   *   *

He sat at the kitchen table in the morning. The leaves had turned, and the air was chilly, though not uncomfortable. The maid threw another piece of kindling into the kitchen hearth. There was coffee, bread, eggs, pineapple and cheesecake. "Eat," Mary said. Theodore wasn't hungry, however. He rose from the table abruptly and grabbed his hat and coat. "There are certain business matters that need immediate attention," he said, exiting the back door of his residence.

Mary shook her head as the maid wiped the table. Her husband was growing more and more distracted.

CHAPTER FIFTY-THREE

Theodore sat in his office at the *Connecticut Courant*. He was the newspaper's editor, and he spent as much time overseeing the running of the paper as he did practicing law. Ezekiel Hood worked in an adjoining room at a separate press. He was running off pamphlets concerning the growing rumors that President Jefferson was sleeping with several of his slaves, a practice which had begun, according to some, when he was envoy to Paris. This was shameful, and Theodore believed it was his duty to tell people of Jefferson's horrific behavior lest the President be re-elected the following year, in 1804.

He had also produced many pamphlets regarding Jefferson's ongoing use of the patronage system. Elizur Goodrich, brother of Chauncey Goodrich, had been removed from the collectorship of New Haven years before, in the Adams' administration. There had been other examples of this indefensible behavior, of course, but this was the case that Theodore could not remove from his mind. Any threat to the Goodrich family was not to be tolerated. Should Chauncey be troubled in any way, his ability to control his wife Marianne might be jeopardized. Chauncey was a good and decent man—the two talked on many occasions—and Theodore privately felt that Chauncey Goodrich, a man of strong character, was the only thing which prevented adultery from decimating his household. Theodore's dreams were clear on this point: adultery was always a danger to any marriage, but he could not bear the thought of Marianne straying from her husband. Theodore himself had perhaps contributed to her character flaws years before, and he did not know what he would do should she not steer a perfect moral course.

But there was more which Theodore had to do on this particular morning. He intended to reprint his poem "Moll Carey," which had originally appeared in pamphlet form. The poem depicted the scene of a drunken Jeffersonian festival in New Haven in March, 1803. Moll Carey was the owner of a brothel in New York City. Dwight placed a motley crew of Jeffersonian liberals on the Green in New Haven all of them gambling, whoring and drinking. As an added touch, he had added a character with the nickname of Old Porpoise, an unsavory man modeled after his Uncle Pierpont, a man fallen into misery and sin because of adultery and the influence of the French.

*   *   *

"How are the headaches?" asked Mason, sitting across from Theodore in the office of the *Courant*.

"I find that they are alleviated only by work," confessed Theodore.

"As both your friend and doctor, I was going to advise, as usual, that you take time to relax once in a while," said Mason.

"So you have said to me three or four hundred times.

But this country will perish without diligence."

"Federalism will survive with or without Theodore Dwight," said Mason. "Our candidates still hold their own at election time. We have our victories—we have our defeats. The Alien Enemies Act prevented many of the French from emigrating to our shores, thus preventing them from becoming loyal party members of Jefferson. The Sedition Act stopped many of the existing Jeffersonians from expressing their views openly. We do what we can."

Theodore rose and paced back and forth. "The damned French," he said. "Jefferson can claim neutrality between the French and British all he wants, but the bastard has been in bed with France for years now. He might as well sleep with Bonaparte himself. Britain is our mother country, Mason. It has discipline and reason." He turned to face Cogswell. "We're simply not doing enough."

"I share your concerns, Theodore. But a man is, after all is said and done, composed of memories. The present moment lasts but an infinitesimal second, and then it is gone. Make sure that Theodore Dwight has good memories to look back on. My prescription for you, my dear friend, is a glass of brandy tonight as you sit in a comfortable chair."

Theodore smiled. He appreciated his friend's concerns, and he respected his advice. He did not agree, however, with the opinion that Federalism would survive without Theodore Dwight. In his own mind, *he* was Federalism. His own party members too often abandoned their principles. They had not voted for Thomas Pinckney, for example, thus allowing the detestable Mr. Jefferson to become the Vice President of John Adams in an election which Theodore could not forget even though it was seven years in the past.

The kingdom of God would not be established on earth as long as men like Jefferson were able to control the destinies of men. To say that Jefferson was the anti-Christ would not be an exaggeration.

*   *   *

"Watch, Theodore," said Jefferson as he lowered his body onto Mary Ogden. "I'll show you the proper technique of lovemaking."

Theodore tried to back away. He felt waves of revulsion spreading throughout his body. He was nauseated, dizzy, disoriented. He wanted to turn away, but he couldn't—he was in the firm grasp of Uncle Pierpont.

"Stop, you French-loving bastard!" Theodore cried.

When Jefferson had finished with Mary, he was joined by Marianne, Abigail, and Ann, his brother's wife. All were naked.

There was an orgy in the bedroom of Mary Ogden; likewise, there was an orgy in America. Men and women had lost their bearings.

Theodore cried out, terrified that the world might be at an end. Could things get any worse? Surely the Apocalypse had arrived.

"Shhh," said Mary, putting her arms around her husband.

"My head," he groaned. "The pain is unendurable." This had been his worst nightmare ever.

"I shall make it better," Mary promised, drawing

Theodore even closer. She hummed softly, rocking her husband gently until he fell back asleep.

CHAPTER FIFTY-FOUR

A man is composed of memories.

This was true, Theodore thought as he approached the gathering of delegates in Hartford on December 15, 1814. He had been the editor of the *Connecticut Mirror*, and he had written dozens of articles expounding the Federalist cause. He had served in the national congress briefly, from 1806 to 1807, filling a seat left vacant by the resignation of John Cotton Smith. He had agreed to serve in order to firm up his party to the extent that such could be done while the country was in the hands of the abominable Mr. Jefferson, who was far more interested in his image as statesman than in the actual practice of government. He had watched his son, Theodore Junior start to mature into a young man of principle and integrity. He had watched his dutiful wife tend to the daily chores of their home with quiet pride and dignity. More than anything, perhaps, he had watched leaves fall. In October and November of each year, he loved to sit outside his home for hours at a time, watching the dried, multi-colored leaves fall to the ground. Sometimes he even counted the individual leaves gathered at his feet, and when enough of them had accumulated, he started all over again. It was a simple occupation, and next to an occasional glass of brandy, was the most efficacious remedy for his crippling headaches.

But there were new memories waiting to made now, memories waiting to form inside the convention hall where Federalist delegates would discuss the deportment of the War of 1812, known among Theodore and his associates as Mr. Madison's War. President Madison had succeeded Jefferson, and it was doubtful if he would have been elected without the issue of a war to bolster his rather weak and pathetic personality. He was simply Jefferson wearing a different suit of clothes—a view he had expressed in several orations, pamphlets, and newspaper articles.

Theodore was the secretary of the Hartford Convention, and while there were those people who thought Theodore Dwight was disrespectful in his satirical writings, he was an important man within his party. His job as secretary was proof, was it not?

He entered the assembly, the hall inside noisy with the echo of so many voices which had yet to be summoned to order by George Cabot, who was presiding over the gathering.

*   *   *

Hours later, Theodore found himself thoroughly bored. There had been many speeches punctuated by bursts of applause or, in some cases, rude shouts of approval or disagreement from the delegates. There was much talk about the impressment of American seaman by the British navy, which had been going on for some time. To Theodore, impressment was not something that should have concerned Jefferson or Madison; Britain needed able-bodied men to fight the French in the European theater. Stopping the French was paramount. Indeed, he did not understand why more Americans didn't volunteer outright to aid Great Britain.

Erastus had been correct in his thinking from the very beginning. Britain stood for order—it always had, and it always would. It was a God-fearing nation, and even in his madness, Erastus understood this all too well. If the United States did not want to aid Great Britain directly years earlier, attempting to remain neutral in the dispute between France and England, how could Great Britain be blamed for the actions it had taken on the seas?

America's constant flirtation with the French—whether overt or clandestine—was adultery. Jefferson's soul was black with whoring, both politically and personally, and his damnation in the next life was a *fait accompli* as far as Theodore was concerned.

The speeches droned on. The other speakers thus far were not addressing the heart of the matter at this convention in Hartford.

* * *

It was the following day, when Theodore met with John Lowell and Timothy Pickering. Dwight felt that the convention might be properly focused on the paramount issue, which was on everyone's mind . . . the one that no one had directly addressed as of yet: the possibility of the New England states making a separate peace with Great Britain—the possibility of secession.

"Are you with us?" Lowell asked Theodore in a small room where the three men were alone.

"Yes." That was all he said. He didn't need to hesitate or qualify his response. The word was on his tongue, ready to be articulated.

Pickering nodded approvingly. "We have several dozen delegates who are ready to commit to secession and many more who are remaining silent despite their obvious sympathies with us. There are very few people here willing to commit our state militias to a fight with the British."

"Such a use of our men is clearly unconstitutional," said Theodore. "There is no imminent threat of invasion."

"Let the *southern* states forfeit their men if they choose," said Lowell sarcastically.

Pickering paced back and forth. He was clearly disturbed despite the agreement he and his colleague had found in the convention's secretary. "There is an even larger issue," he stated, "that I fear we cannot debate publicly with complete candor."

He paused, his face etched with grave lines of deliberation.

"We have reached a point," he continued, "at which I think the republic, as it now stands, is irredeemable. I fear we have sold our souls. Or perhaps I should say that the Democratic-Republicans have *taken* our souls and given them away. This is not the Union of Washington or Adams. It is a politically divisive country. We can continue to battle Jefferson's puppets . . . or we can start over again. The Revolution itself is our precedent."

Theodore rose from his chair. "We have become an atheist country," he proclaimed. "The light of scripture no longer shines on this land, which has been defiled."

"How exactly shall we proceed, gentlemen?"

questioned Lowell.

Dwight put a hand on each man's shoulder. "I have quite a bit of experience in coercion and in working behind the scenes for our party. The manner in which this subject is broached should be subtle. If handled correctly, our opinions here this morning will spread like wildfire."

Lowell and Pickering were interested in results, not methods. They exited the room, leaving Theodore to devise a means whereby the delegates could be persuaded to act upon their bold proposal.

*   *   *

Theodore approached Harrison Gray Otis after lunch. Otis was a moderate, but Theodore believed that the key to the success of Pickering's plan was to convince the more hesitant delegates, men like Otis, who were a bit too cautious unless prodded by the right argument. Otis was staring out the window of the same room where Theodore had met with Lowell and Pickering earlier in the day. The day was freezing cold but sunny, and standing in the patch of sun painted across the hardwood floor was pleasant.

"Our daughters have been raped," said Theodore quietly.

Harrison, a middle-aged man dressed in a gray coat, turned slowly to look at his companion. His deep-set eyes were filled with skepticism. "I don't believe I heard you correctly," said Harrison.

"I think you did," said Theodore calmly. "Our daughters have been raped by members of Mr. Madison's party. Few here speak about it openly. The Democratic-

Republicans believe they are exempt from certain codes of behavior. They have no respect for our children."

"I have a daughter," said Otis, "and I assure you that she has not been touched in any questionable manner." He seemed quite angry at Theodore's assertion.

"Perhaps not yet," said Theodore cautiously. "But her time will come if we do not distance ourselves morally from these lecherous men."

Otis left the room, slamming the door behind him.

Theodore had no qualms about making such an accusation. The minds of people were continually being corrupted by Jefferson's party. To subject the minds of young people to atheism and lust was to violate those minds.

It was the moral equivalent of rape.

*   *   *

Theodore spoke to many other delegates over the next few days, one at a time, always in private, always in a guarded tone of voice. He spoke of the self-serving interests of Madison and Monroe. He spoke of secret meetings which he knew for a fact—or so he said—Jefferson had held with Bonaparte while president. And he spoke continually about the political corruptibility of the Democratic-Republicans.

He told others the story of how his father's farm was ransacked when he was a boy. If the New England states released their militias, who would be there to defend New England in case there really *was* an invasion which threatened the peace and security of farms and residences?

"The nation must be saved from adultery," he told

others, "or Moll Carey and her prostitutes will overtake us all."

*   *   *

The convention ended three weeks later. There would be no secession. Madison's conduct was exonerated. Various amendments were proposed that would redress certain grievances of the northern states, but otherwise no action was to be taken. Moreover, Andrew Jackson managed a glorious victory in New Orleans to close the war. The Hartford Convention had ended abruptly.

Very few of the delegates spoke to Dwight as they left the meeting hall on the final day, January 4, 1815. Some sneered at him; others brushed past him without acknowledgment.

It was Harrison Otis who spoke to him straightforwardly. "Your services have perhaps been valued too highly by our party," he said. "Leave matters in the hands of others, Mr. Dwight. Your odd sense of humor is wearing thin on many of us. Perhaps you are more suited for the clergy."

"My brother was the president of Yale!" replied Theodore angrily. This statement had nothing whatsoever to do with Otis's statement, but it was the only thing which came to Theodore's mind.

"Your brother," said Otis, "is a gentleman. You, sir, are an ass."

CHAPTER FIFTY-FIVE

Theodore lived in great pain for the next few months. His headaches were constant. A political pamphlet was nailed to his front door, depicting him with donkey ears. He was not able to practice law, so thoroughly had his spirits and hopes been deflated. The Treaty of Ghent had ended the War of 1812, without a single word on impressment, which had been the strongest reason given for military engagement in the first place. James Madison was a hero. The mood in Connecticut, as in most of New England, was that the nation had endured despite its internal conflicts. For the most part, there was no appetite for exposing the moral deficiencies of Madison and Jefferson.

Theodore and Mary decided to move to Albany, New York, where he would become editor of the *Albany Daily Advertiser*. He needed distance from Hartford. Perhaps in Albany he could carry on his work. His wit was sharp, and he could still write.

* * *

Much of the Dwights' belongings had been sent ahead to Albany. A few matters remained, such as the closing of his law practice. Theodore walked down the street absentmindedly as he made his way home from his office.

"Why Theodore, how pleasant it is to see you," said a soft voice.

It was Marianne Goodrich.

"Good evening, Mrs. Goodrich," replied Theodore courteously.

"I hear you shall be leaving us for Albany soon. May I take this opportunity to wish you all the best?"

"Thank you very much," Theodore said, bowing. "You are so very kind."

He walked on, but he could feel that Marianne was still looking at him, having expected him to say something more since he was leaving town. But he could not bring himself to make any more pleasantries. Even after all the years which had passed, dreams of Marianne still crept into his sleeping brain. Whenever a candle was lit or a fire blazed in the hearth, he knew that the shadow of Jonathan Edwards was watching him.

He wished he had not seen Marianne on the street. She was still so pretty. He knew he would have more dreams in the next several months.

*   *   *

"Farewell," said Mason Fitch as Theodore and Mary stood next to the coach which would deliver them from Hartford to Albany.

Goodbye," said Theodore. "You're a good man, Mason. I value your friendship as I value no other. Write to me in Albany."

"Theodore Dwight is also a good man," declared Fitch, "though I believe he is a bit too hard on himself."

"We must be hard on ourselves, my dear Mason, lest God himself be harsh with us on judgment day."

The coach rumbled down Asylum street until it disappeared in the dust from its rear wheels. It was late April, 1815 and the Dwight's would be settled into their new home in Albany, New York within a month.

New York,
1815-

Chapter Fifty-Six

Albany   December 20, 1815
My Dear Mason,
How far the Democrats are sick of me, I am not able to say. The will of the Secretary of the Hartford Convention, which a short time ago glared in almost every democratic paper in the country, has subsided. Here they are quite silent, finding me something like the Rhode Island hedgehog—not to be tamed, thwarted, nor coaxed. I am obliged to fight accusatory warfare.

Remember us affectionately to Mrs. Cogswell and the children; and to such of our old neighbors as inquire of us. We think of them with great regard.

I am most surely and affectionately yours—

Theodore Dwight

Mason would, without a doubt, understand that Theodore meant for him to relay his best wishes to Marianne Goodrich. Now that he was separated from Marianne by a considerable physical distance, his thoughts had eased considerably. His headaches had almost disappeared. He regretted being so curt the last time he had encountered

Marianne, especially since she had been so kind in wishing him well before his departure. But Mason, having read his letters for so many years, would be able to decipher his oblique message.

Life was quiet now for Theodore. He would never give up his Federalist beliefs—indeed, as he had told Mason, he would continue to fight accusatory warfare—but the immediate political burdens had been lifted from his shoulders. He would write. Most of all, he would observe the nation, taking its moral pulse whenever necessary. He was, after all, the vehicle of the Most High, an instrument of God on earth. He would not lose faith, nor would he allow people to forget that government must serve the cause of morality and order. If he needed to make accusations, it would be done in the cause of righteousness.

Even Theodore's nightmares began to dissipate. His most prevalent dream was of steering a boat down a wide silver river. His wife and five children were his passengers. He knew exactly how to navigate the waters. At times a thunderstorm appeared on the horizon, the wind sending first ripples and then waves against the bow of the longboat. His wife Mary would cringe, sometimes even hiding her head under the canvas which protected their goods. Thunder always scared her so. But Theodore did not falter in his guidance. "Do not doubt, ye of little faith," he would tell his family.

The boat always passed safely through the storm.

*   *   *

A man who has children is a man who finds that the

years grow shorter with each turn of the seasons. It had been a long time since Theodore had looked up from the grave of Reverend May's granddaughter and noticed the bare limbs of a tree, but he still sat in his yard on many occasions, counting the bits of leaf-meal drifting down to the ground near his feet. Each leaf seemed to represent a newspaper article for the *Albany Daily Advertiser*, a letter to Mason, a gray hair, a new presidential election.

Erastus had died, although Cecil and Ann now had four children.

Mr. and Mrs. Goodrich also had children. This gave Theodore particular satisfaction. His longing for Clarinda seemed to belong to a different lifetime, a different Theodore Dwight.

And still the leaves fell from the trees, and Theodore learned that his mother had died, and for months he brooded, feeling gray in his soul.

But his wife Mary was always at his side when his spirits darkened. She would hold him at night, gently reminding him that his duties were not yet finished in this world.

It was Mary, in fact, who was the first to tell her husband of the news he had waited such a long time to hear. "Jefferson has died," she said.

It was 1826, and Theodore suddenly realized what an important task God was calling him to.

He became a man driven, a man who would get up earlier than usual so that he might journey to New York or Washington or Hartford. He needed to collect every written word he could find about Jefferson, especially Jefferson's *own* words—his speeches, his letters, his essays. It would make Theodore's accusatory warfare so much easier.

*   *   *

The years slipped by like yellow afternoon sunlight creeping quietly along a stone wall. Theodore now measured the days by how many pages he had written, pages of books which would not only give the people of the United States a moral compass, but also a true understanding of people and events that he himself had lived through, events that he himself had participated in.

At times his hand was too cramped to write another word. These were the times when Jonathan Edwards, sitting in some shadowy corner, urged his grandson on. "Run the good race," he would tell Theodore, quoting St. Paul. "Your mission is not yet done."

It is the older man who takes the greatest notice of the angle of the sun, perhaps because he has acquired the understanding that the sun will only rise and set so many times in a person's life.

Such a man was Theodore Dwight, and he was exceedingly happy as the sun measured his days.

Theodore Dwight died on June 12, 1846. He can be remembered as a political extremist. Historian David Hackett Fisher said that Dwight's pamphleteering "was marked by some of the most outrageous – but incisive-scurrility in the annals of the republic." Politically rabid, Dwight alienated some people in his own party. By 1818 the Federalist Party virtually disappeared. His fixation on

Jefferson was in the end excessive, although there were other, prominent New Englanders who shared Dwight's views about Jefferson, including Chief Justice, Joseph Storey. But for Dwight there was also a personal, psychological component to his antipathy; Jefferson became an outward manifestation of Dwight's own inner demons.

Jefferson symbolized the local revolutionaries who ransacked his family's farm and precipitated the untimely demise of his father. As a thirteen year-old boy Dwight was helpless as his family was terrorized by local revolutionaries. Without a father for guidance Dwight went through an extended adolescence seeking solace and fulfillment in romance. In fact, he developed a reputation as a rake and perhaps a drinker. He then found direction through the guidance of Reverend May and purpose through a new found belief in God and scripture. By trying to prevent the ascendancy of Jefferson, Dwight was somehow getting back at the revolutionaries who ransacked his family farm. By pointing out Jefferson's lust and moral transgressions, Dwight was coming to terms with his own. But Dwight's life was much more than this.

Chauncey Goodrich married Marianne Wolcott (Clarinda) and one of their sons, Samuel, wrote about Dwight in his book, *Recollections of Lifetime.* He said that Dwight was an example of man who was wicked in the political realm, but was the "milk of kindness at home." Much of what Dwight wrote as a partisan pamphleteer was "curing a public taste for ridiculous bombast, which then prevailed." What's important is that Dwight was a wonderful father of 12 children. His children all did well. In fact, Theodore Dwight Junior was a leading abolitionist; it was no mistake that his father wrote the first anti-slavery poem in America. Theodore Dwight was an accomplished, good man, but also human.

www.ingramcontent.com/pod-product-compliance
Lightning Source LLC
Chambersburg PA
CBHW022004160426
43197CB00007B/274